The Outreaching Church

Growing Beyond the Walls

By
Mac Mayer

THE OUTREACHING CHURCH

Growing Beyond the Walls

MAC MAYER

The Outreaching Church
By Mac Mayer

Copyright ©2022 by Mac Mayer

All rights reserved. For use of any part of this publication, whether reproduced, transmitted in any form or by any means, electronic, mechanical, photocopying, recording, or otherwise, or stored in a retrieval system, without the prior consent of the publisher, is an infringement of copyright law and is forbidden. Names have been changed to protect the privacy of the individuals involved in the stories or scenarios. All other stories are composites of the lives of real people and any similarities to people you may know are purely coincidental.

The author and Endurance Press shall have neither liability nor responsibility to any person or entity with respect to loss, damage, or injury caused or alleged to be caused directly or indirectly by the information contained in this book. The information presented herein is in no way intended as a substitute for counseling and other forms of professional guidance.

To contact the author for speaking engagements, or for more information, you can access his website at www.macmayer.com.

Scripture quotations marked (KJV) are taken from the King James Version Bible. The KJV is public domain in the United States.

Scripture quotations taken from The Holy Bible, New

International Version® NIV®. Copyright © 1973 1978 1984 2011 by Biblica, Inc.™ Used by permission. All rights reserved worldwide.

Scripture taken from the New King James Version®. Copyright © 1982 by Thomas Nelson. Used by permission. All rights reserved.

Scripture quotations marked (ESV) are from the ESV® Bible (The Holy Bible, English Standard Version®), copyright © 2001 by Crossway, a publishing ministry of Good News Publishers. Used by permission. All rights reserved.

Scripture quotations marked (NLT) are taken from the Holy Bible, New Living Translation, copyright ©1996, 2004, 2015 by Tyndale House Foundation. Used by permission of Tyndale House Publishers, Carol Stream, Illinois 60188. All rights reserved.

Cover Design: Anurup Ghosh
Interior Design: Robert Sweesy, Endurance Press

Print ISBN: 978-1-7363842-4-4

First Printing 2022
Printed in the United States of America
Published by Endurance Press

Contents

Acknowledgments 9

Preface 11

Introduction 13

Chapter 1: Unfulfilled 16

Chapter 2: Two Problems, One Solution 29

Chapter 3: Who Is in the House? 40

Chapter 4: Structured for Success 55

Chapter 5: What Is in Your Hand? 68

Chapter 6: Change Your Focus 80

Chapter 7: What Are You Going to Say? 97

Chapter 8: A Scalable Biblical Model 120

Chapter 9: Get in the Game 138

Acknowledgments

I'm incredibly thankful for the Holy Spirit's coauthoring in this writing process. As I'm praying, thinking, and writing books, I'm always overwhelmed by the magnitude of what the Holy Spirit is teaching me. I'm VERY thankful for the Holy Spirit's willingness to teach, share, and assist me in this process. Thank You! I pray for His guidance and direction as you use this information to tangibly change lives outside your church for the Kingdom.

Also, a GIGANTIC thanks to the amazing women in my life. To my God-addicted wife, whom I had the good fortune to marry over 30 years ago. Dianne has allowed me to be who I am, and she sets an example of passionately following God. Miss Jenny is the next amazing lady in our world. Jenny is like a daughter to Dianne and me; she has the unenviable job of overseeing what I've been trying to accomplish for the last 20 years. A special shout-out also goes to Miss Marce, who is assigned to keep track of me daily at Life Church. Now that's a challenge, and she surpasses all expectations.

Dianne and I have been very fortunate to have amazing godly couples in our lives. Pastor Lynn and Dorette Schaal of Twin Falls, Idaho, were great examples in our early years fol-

The Outreaching Church

lowing Christ. They are a wonderful God-following couple. A special acknowledgment goes to Pastor Mark and Amy Boer. I think a little differently than others—okay, a lot differently—and they had the patience and understanding to allow me to find my way while setting an incredible example of a couple who is 100% committed to following God.

Preface

I have two major passions in life. The first is to help individuals understand that God has a plan for their lives and to help them discover it. My second is helping churches grow. The cool thing for me is that these passions are intertwined. As churches develop ways for individual believers to find and fulfill God's plan for their lives, churches start growing! I'm a church growth junkie. I read about church growth, talk about church growth, pray about church growth, and yes, I even dream about church growth. However, I'm not just interested in growing the church I attend; I'm interested in assisting all churches that represent Jesus to flourish.

This book follows the foundation laid by three previous books and is devoted to helping people find God's plan for their life while building outreach ministries to impact their communities for Christ. This will result in—you guessed it—church growth. The other three books have related information that develops the base from which to build outreach ministries.

My first nonbusiness book, *Well Done*, describes achieving the ultimate success as a Christian. It details the *why* of what we do, which is to hear, "Well done, thou good and faithful servant" (Matthew 25:21a, KJV), resulting in

The Outreaching Church

glory being given to Jesus. My next book, *The Empowered Church*, describes the biblical truth every church can use to create an operating structure for optimal growth—the *how* of church growth. The third book is *The Connected Church*, which describes the growth metrics that every church should know. I talk about strategies for increasing those numbers that result in lives eternally changed and discipled, which is *what* we do that results in solid church growth.

One of the main concepts in *The Connected Church* is developing outreach ministries. This is an area most churches struggle with and don't understand, but it is essential for growth. I felt compelled to write specifically about this subject because so few churches understand how to do it or the impact it will make in their church. A church serving its community for Christ is outward-focused. This results in a healthy, thriving church larger on the outside of its walls than on the inside.

Introduction

There seems to be a current weird paradox of problems that, on the surface, seem unrelated. On one side, the world seems overwhelmed with issues: the pandemic, struggling businesses, widespread isolation. Then there is the issue of dropping church attendance, closing churches, and the church being less influential in society and people's lives. Many people I talk to feel as I once did—unfulfilled. Many of us believe it is an advantage to attend church and that our lives are better for it, but a nagging emptiness and haunting questions are reverberating in our minds.

Isn't there more to our spiritual life than coming to a church every week, being a spectator, watching other people use their gifts for Kingdom influence? Isn't there something more we can do to impact lives for the Kingdom?

My ambitious goal in this book is to create a guide for a chain reaction. First, churches understand and develop a simple process so typical attendees can play a significant role in utilizing their God-given gifts to serve humanity. Everyone has the potential to influence others for Christ, and when they have simple steps to do this, great things happen for you, your church, and the Kingdom. The result is a reenergized church empowering the people inside its walls to

The Outreaching Church

impact lives outside the building. When this happens, your church will be an indispensable force serving your community, larger on the outside than it is on the inside.

Mac Mayer

Chapter 1: Unfulfilled

"Father, I feel so unfulfilled! I'm not doing anything for the Kingdom. All I'm doing is making money. Father, I want to do something to affect lives for you!"

To be honest, my outburst was 90% complaining and 10% praying. I was frustrated and discontent. It was a warm, sunny day, and I was driving through our town after viewing one of our investment properties. I realized I had accomplished what "they" said would make me happy, yet I was miserable. I was making money and achieving all the things the world said I should accomplish, but the result was emptiness and discouragement.

My wife and I owned several businesses, had a home in the country, even a second home at a resort. We had all the trappings of success. We had the toys, nice cars, investment properties, ability to travel, and none of it brought me real contentment. I felt like I was living a life of quiet desperation. As a business owner, I would come to church every week and listen to the pastor who was fulfilling the call of God on his life, but I felt like a spectator, not in the game. Does any of this sound familiar or relate to you?

Things have dramatically changed since that pivotal day and plea for help. Thankfully, I'm now able to use my skill sets to grow the Kingdom of God. I make less money, but I'm much happier and more fulfilled as I help individuals and churches succeed in impacting their communities. My biggest nightmare would be to go back to my old lifestyle when I wasn't using the abilities God gave me for Kingdom purposes. Everything I did was all about me and the accumulation of stuff. I'm so thankful to God for allowing me to use my talents for Him. The great news is—so can you!

I talk with ordinary churchgoers all the time. These are just regular people like you and me. They are business owners, employees, husbands, wives, and single people. They all seem to have a universal question or thought, and it goes something like this:

> What about me? Is there something that I can do for the Kingdom? I know my pastor is doing what he is supposed to, but I don't feel called to be a pastor. So is there anything I can do? I feel like I am just a spectator watching the game of life go by, and I don't feel important. I am not involved in or part of what God is doing. Is there anything for me?

I have great news for you. Yes, God has a plan for your life, and you can find it. I'm praying this book will help you on your journey to find real Kingdom fulfillment.

You will read real-life accounts of ordinary people who are now fulfilling God's plan for their life and how you can do the same. If you don't know what God has for you, you will find help on your journey to discover it. My goal is to encourage the body of Christ to rise up to take its rightful place in society because everyone has a vital role helping both thrive. I want to help you make your church larger on the outside than on the inside.

Pastors and church leaders will find help in creating an operating structure that will include their whole congregation in what God is doing. Regular (non-pastoral) people looking for options will discover a game plan for them to fulfill what God has placed on their hearts. Your community will be impacted, and your church will be growing and healthy, accomplishing what God has commanded us to do: go and make disciples of all nations. Best of all, you will be fulfilled knowing you are an active part of the success while accomplishing what God designed you to do.

One Prayer

If you had only one prayer to change the world, and the answer was guaranteed, what would it be?

I don't know what you think about current events, but to me, it appears that the whole world is totally jacked up, with problems galore and record-breaking levels of insanity everywhere. It doesn't matter which way you turn; chaos abounds. As I write this book, here in the US there is a mess at the southern border, a worldwide pandemic, runaway inflation, propagated racism, and gender confusion. There are companies needing workers and workers not able to work or even being paid to stay home. Inventory is lowering and gas prices are soaring. This doesn't even consider questionable elections and trillions of dollars in overspending. Jesus, take the wheel! Hopefully, by the time you read this, some of these issues will be resolved, but there will likely be a whole new set of problems headed to our doorsteps to replace them.

So, if you could have one prayer answered that would make a difference in this crazy time, what would it be? With the laundry list barely scratching the surface, I can get overwhelmed with what to pray about. There are just so many issues!

After a significant amount of time praying and reflecting on what to pray about, I rested on this one single prayer: that the whole body of Christ, all the followers of Jesus, would step up. I pray we would take our proper place of serving society, utilizing the talents and abilities God has placed in us to influence the world for good. This is what Jesus talked about in the Parable of the Talents in Matthew 25. I believe that when we, as the body of Christ, seek what God would have us do and do it, great things will happen! We have Jesus! That means we have the ability to solve society's most profound problems.

If this makes sense to you, would you also pray with me for the body of Christ to step up and be the answer society is looking for? Actually, let's not just pray but also personally DO what God has called us to. Let's unite, take our place, and **be the answer**.

God's Crazy, Amazing Love

If we are going to change the world, it will take substantial horsepower. After all, it took a pile of people working overtime to mess the place up. I recently saw a bumper sticker that said, "Jesus is coming back. Look busy!" The concept is funny because God is not a wicked taskmaster, and our eternal salvation has nothing to do with works. On the other hand, if I understand how much God loves me, I should be busy.

Let's ponder the magnitude of God's love. God created Adam in His image to be an eternal companion to Him. God watched Adam make the horrible choice to disobey Him (aka sin), resulting in Adam's and ultimately all of mankind's separation from God. This separation broke God's heart because Adam and his descendants would be apart from Him forever. So our loving Father developed this amazingly elaborate plan that took thousands of years to fulfill: He/God would be placed as a seed in the womb of a mortal virgin woman. This God/man baby named Jesus came to earth to live a sinless life as a man and to pay the ultimate penalty of our sin. The cost of our sin was the torture and crucifixion of God's own sinless Son who took our place.

The crazy, profound truth is God became a man so He could die for us. He paid the ultimate price because of His incredible love. If I truly understand what God has done for me, I don't need to act busy; I will gladly be about my loving Father's business, with a heart full of gratitude, thankfulness, and love.

Once we realize the incredible blessing of Jesus, we just can't be idle. As a friend of mine likes to say, "If you don't think what Jesus did for us is too good to be true, you really don't understand what He did." When we understand this marvelous plan and God's love for us, it is humbling and an honor to serve Him in any way that we can.

Everyone Has a Ministry

We already know that it is important to pray for the body of Christ to step up, and we also need to discover what God would have each of us do and accomplish it. My viewpoint is this: we all have a ministry. Don't check out on me! You don't have to spend four years in a Bible college or have "Rev." in front of your name in order to have a ministry. You don't have to go to another country or learn a foreign language.

The Greek word generally translated as "ministry" in the New Testament is *diakonia*. This word simply means "service."[1] In Second Corinthians 5:17–21, Paul writes,

---

[1] Bible Hub, s.v. "diakonia," accessed December 28, 2021, https://biblehub.com/greek/1249.htm.

The Outreaching Church

Therefore, if anyone is in Christ, the new creation has come: The old has gone, the new is here! All this is from God, who reconciled us to himself through Christ and gave us the ministry of reconciliation: that God was reconciling the world to himself in Christ, not counting people's sins against them. And he has committed to us the message of reconciliation. We are therefore Christ's ambassadors, as though God were making his appeal through us. We implore you on Christ's behalf: Be reconciled to God. God made him who had no sin to be sin for us, so that in him we might become the righteousness of God. (NIV)

We are called to the ministry of reconciliation. What does that mean? It simply means that we help others and show them the love of Jesus through our acts of service. Everyone has the potential to influence others for Christ, thereby leading them to reconciliation with God.

We all have a personal testimony of how our lives were influenced for God. In virtually every story, this happened through other people and our association with them. We don't come to a saving knowledge of Jesus in a vacuum; other people have a part to play. My life was the same. I grew up in a middle-income family in a small town in Idaho. Unfortunately, our family was influenced by abundant alcohol consumption, resulting in a myriad of dysfunctional behaviors. I had a driven, rebellious personality, which didn't help matters, and at 16, I left school and home. With little education, I had several meager low-paying jobs.

By the grace of God, at 18 years old and through crazy circumstances, I heard real estate appraisers were needed, and anybody could start a company with no qualifications. I seemed to fit the description, so I opened an appraisal company with no knowledge or experience. That worked, so I started five different companies by the time I was 20 years old. The only problem was that all the dysfunction planted in me while growing up was reaping a bountiful harvest of craziness in my life. I started taking on the very attributes I had hated growing up.

Not only was I living out some of the worst aspects of my childhood, but the power of association was also working against me. In brief, this principle says, "You are like those you hang around." At that time, my associations were terrible! My best friend went to prison for eight years. Growing up, I did not have a single friend who had a good relationship with their dad.

I became a workaholic and worked massive hours and began making piles of money. Unfortunately, I had the maturity of a doorknob, which is a recipe for a screwed-up life. I could tell you some hair-raising stories, but let's leave it at this—I was a poster child for dysfunction, and I hated it. So what changed?

The Outreaching Church

The answer is: I met Christian businessmen. These men had all the attributes I had not experienced in my childhood and teen years. They were sober, happily married, and their kids liked them. I was in awe. These men lived their lives and ran their businesses as a ministry. I was drawn to them, even though nothing in my lifestyle reflected Christian values. For years they demonstrated caring and patience with me. I finally saw the truth and accepted Jesus. I will be eternally thankful for these men. I'm sure I wouldn't be alive today without their influence.

Even though I had accepted Jesus, my lifestyle didn't reflect this new truth. I needed continued association with good people to help me mature in my thoughts and actions. Paul says that we should not be conformed to the pattern of this world, but "be transformed by the renewing of your mind" (Romans 12:2, NIV). This is best done in community with others. My wife and I joined a small group led by a bank manager and his wife. This couple became an incredible example for Dianne and me in our relationship with one another. I'm positive we wouldn't be married today without their influence and that of many other Christians. These men and women lived their lives like a ministry in order to serve and impact those around them, and we were the benefactors.

I was influenced for Christ through Christians who seemed to have the answers I was looking for. My personal life was a train wreck. I didn't want to perpetuate my childhood in another generation. I was looking for a solution to my problems. Isn't that the way it worked in your life? We all moved forward to become a Christian to solve a deep need. Maybe it was the reality of eternity. Maybe it was that we didn't have peace. Perhaps our life was off the rails, and we just wanted to put an end to the craziness. In any case, becoming a Christian represented an answer to something we were dealing with.

Now we have the opportunity to pass on the solution of Jesus to others. We, as Christians, can be significant, positive influencers to those around us. God has gifted us with abilities and talents that are the answers to the needs of people in the world. As Paul wrote to the church at Ephesus, "For we are His workmanship, created in Christ Jesus for good works, which God prepared beforehand that we should walk in them" (Ephesians 2:10, NKJV). When we have answers, it allows us to point people to Jesus. Let's talk about how this works.

The Power of Proximity

Robert H. Schuller once said, "The secret of success is to find a need and fill it, to find a hurt and heal it, to find somebody with a problem and offer to help solve it."[2] When we talk about the ultimate of all success, leading others to Jesus and one day hearing, "Well done, thou good and faithful servant" from our Master, this idea of healing hurts and solving problems is essential. Your talents and abilities

---
2   "Robert H. Schuller Quotes," Quotefancy.com, accessed 05/17/2022, https://quotefancy.com/robert-h-schuller-quotes.

can be the answer to someone's needs. Solving their needs creates proximity because people are drawn to you.

Proximity leads to association and association creates influence. If we can help meet people's needs in a meaningful way, they will continue to be drawn to us. This gives us the opportunity to influence them for Christ. Our mindset should be that every Christian is a potential minister (remember—that means "helper") because *everyone is gifted with the answer to someone else's need.* Bang!

> Proximity leads to association and association creates influence.

The world has problems, and if we have the solution, the world comes to us. If we have food, we can feed the homeless. If we have a skill set and the world needs what we have, they come to us. If you can fix my computer that just crashed, you are my new best friend, and I will listen to you about other things. If you can repair my blown-up engine, you are again another new best friend. People who can help us with solutions to natural issues become important to us, and they earn the credibility to speak into other areas of our lives, including spiritually.

The power of association is related to proximity, which also can be created in small groups. Our close relationships affect how we think, how we speak, and how we act. This is proven over and over in life. The influence of a group is that much stronger due to a larger number of people to relate to and personalities to mesh with. Association is tragically lacking more than ever in this social media age of surface connections. People's need for real community is ever-growing. We'll talk about this more later.

The Outreaching Church

Reflection Questions

1. Reflect on the idea that everyone has a ministry. Have you ever thought of ministry as something every Christian has? Have you thought of yourself as a minister? How have your thoughts or ideas changed after reading this chapter?
2. How has the power of association helped or hindered your walk with God? In what ways have you been influenced by others for Christ?
3. How have those in your circle been influenced by your love for God?

Chapter 2: Two Problems, One Solution

For the majority of unchurched people, there currently seems to be no compelling reason to attend a church. For these people, the church may not appear to offer anything of value. They may have a stereotype of a boring service where a preacher rails against all the wrong things people are doing and strongly infers they should stop doing those things or suffer the fiery consequences. While there may be some truth to this, it doesn't necessarily relate to our present culture, where people see nothing wrong with boldly living unbiblical lifestyles.

In addition, the church continues to face a significant dropout problem, with recent research indicating that an astounding 64% of 18- to 29-year-olds raised in church have withdrawn from church involvement as an adult, some temporarily, and some permanently.[3] If we understand where society is, we can work intelligently with their perceptions to increase our impact in our communities. This doesn't mean watering down the gospel, but it does mean using

---
3   "Church Dropouts Have Risen to 64%--But What about Those Who Stay?," Barna Group, September 4, 2019, https://www.barna.com/research/resilient-disciples/. Information taken from David Kinnaman's *Faith for Exiles: 5 Ways for a New Generation to Follow Jesus in Digital Babylon*.

The Outreaching Church

biblical principles and wisdom for success.

The segment of society termed the Millennials and the following generation, the Z's, have some very fascinating viewpoints. These age groups are committed to making societal changes through their chosen behaviors and decisions. They believe they can recycle and buy from free-trade companies or corporations that donate money back to underprivileged communities, making a tangible difference in people's lives. They see the church as doing little to help a severely messed-up society, but they have also heard that love is supposed to be an essential attribute of who we are. From their standpoint, our failure to meaningfully impact hurting populations is glaringly hypocritical. We say we love people, but they don't see us following through by doing anything relevant to help people in need.

I guess the Millennials and Z's know how little most churches are actually serving their unsaved communities, and they are not impressed with the underwhelming results. Why would this demographic and others be interested in sitting in a building, listening to someone drone on about loving others or being like Jesus without taking action to do so? You're right; they won't and aren't! Maybe you are feeling the same way, inactive and wanting to get in the game. Read on.

I recently spoke with one of my pastor friends who took over a struggling traditional church. He boldly began taking steps to serve his community. Unfortunately, the established congregation was very uncomfortable with living the Bible they claimed to believe and strongly hinted it was time for him to leave. The long-time attendees seemed offended that he wanted to feed the homeless and live what Jesus modeled. I'm probably venting here, but when someone lives as the Bible indicates, their behavior should look different than that of a nonbeliever!

Remember, the religious leaders were the most ardent attackers of Jesus, and He reserved His strongest rebukes for them. The religious leaders were comfortable in their traditions and were not known for living out Micah 6:8: "He has shown you, O mortal, what is good. And what does the Lord require of you? To act justly and to love mercy and to walk humbly with your God" (NIV).

There is an inspiring classic book entitled *In His Steps* by Charles Sheldon, published in 1897. The book is where the phrase, "What would Jesus do?" became famous. I would recommend you read this life-changing novel, and we all get back to reflecting and living what Jesus really would do.

The Dones

Besides the Millennials and Z's, who could be incredible agents for change in the body of Christ, there is another group of inactive believers the traditional church structure has silenced. If you are frustrated and feeling like you are on the sidelines, not accomplishing what God has placed

The Outreaching Church

on your heart, you may find yourself strongly identifying with them. The Dones (as coined by Josh Packard, author of *Church Refugees*) are *millions of people* who have left the church. They have, in effect, said, "We are done with church." The Dones have fascinating traits from which we can learn. Let's see if these sound familiar or are relevant.

1. They were highly active in their church.
2. They did not want to leave the church.
3. They felt stifled by the church structure.[4]

The end result of these three viewpoints is that the Dones quit attending church, taking the talents and abilities God had given them elsewhere. Don't miss this! The Dones were active in their churches. These people were not freeloaders; they were all in for serving. **They didn't want to leave.** They were committed and wanted to see the church flourish. Maybe these people were trying to live like Jesus. The death blow that caused them to jump ship was **stifling church leadership unwilling to change and serve humanity.** These frustrated people felt like it was in their best interest to work outside of the church structure in order to help people. They were done with the church's bureaucracy. They believed they could not accomplish what God wanted them to do within the organized church.

---

[4] Joshua Packard, "Meet the 'Dones,'" *Christianity Today*, accessed February 24, 2022, https://www.christianitytoday.com/pastors/2015/summer-2015/meet-dones.html. Article adapted from *Church Refugees: Sociologists Reveal Why People Are DONE with Church but Not Their Faith* (Group Publishing, 2015).

This is a gigantic indictment against how we do church when people feel they must leave the church so they can fulfill the call of God on their life! Many of the millions of Dones who have left the church have taken their God-given gifts and talents to secular nonprofits. It's revealing that these people felt like they could better care for humanity outside the church with a nonreligious organization than within the church.[5]

Common Theme

Connecting the dots of what these different groups are saying creates a clear picture of what is missing. These individuals are looking for a structure to help others. They want an opportunity to impact lives. If you are reading this book, you may have similar viewpoints.

Is it too weird that we as a church tangibly help people in unfortunate life situations? That we leave our sacred pews to venture out to offer assistance to hurting people who are looking for answers in our communities? Remember what we talked about in the last chapter—if we provide the answers to people's needs, wrapped in the love of Jesus, they can't help but be compelled to come to us. I suppose we could continue to wait in our deserted church services for broken individuals to eventually stumble through our doors, but that doesn't seem to be working out for the majority of churches using this strategy.

---

5   Packard, "Meet the 'Dones.'"

The Outreaching Church

I know there are great churches impacting their communities, but they are too rare. Too many churches have removed themselves from interacting and serving their fellow man. Because Jesus loves people, He helps them. This is our example: love and help. If we don't help, do we really love? Jesus was all about **going**. He went to where broken people were, and He brought answers. Society has many needs, and the church is too often turning its back on these people because their immediate needs are not spiritual.

The church, at large, seems to be saying, "I know you have financial issues, marriage problems, grief, and addictions, but that is not our problem. We are all about doing our weekly church service for God, so unfortunately, it stinks to be you. When you want to talk about God or something that we are interested in, we will be waiting for you at our half-empty church to tell you how much Jesus loves you!"

Maybe this is what James was referring to when he said, "Suppose a brother or a sister is without clothes and daily food. If one of you says to them, 'Go in peace; keep warm and well fed,' but does nothing about their physical needs, what good is it? In the same way, faith by itself, if it is not accompanied by action, is dead" (James 2:15–17, NIV). Not only should we talk about faith, but we should be compelled to go into our communities for the sake of a lost and dying world.

Many churches seem to have the less-than-progressive growth strategy of waiting for lost people to accidentally walk through their doors. While this occasionally works, it is not the example Jesus set for us to follow. Jesus said, "**Go** into all the world" (Mark 16:15, NIV, emphasis mine). Luke 14:23 says, "**Go** out to the highways and hedges and **compel** people to come in, that my house may be filled" (ESV, emphasis mine). Unfortunately, by its actions, the church tells people their troubling situations are not important, but this is clearly not Jesus's heart or directive.

Jesus may have been tempted to stay in the mountains instead of returning to messy people and their problems. He could have just remained in some remote cave and prayed for them. The only problem was that these high-maintenance people were the ones He passionately loved, came to serve, and eventually died for. Truthfully, I was one of those needy, unsaved, gigantically messed-up people. I'm glad He cared about me. How about you?

Yes, Jesus retreated to the hills for times of refreshing and prayer, but then He went to where people were. He went to the lepers; He went to the madman of the Gadarenes; He went to the lady caught in a sin, and He had answers for them all. If Jesus had been selfish, He might have lived His life like many of us, with little frontline interaction with people in need. Maybe He would have had an impenetrable hedge of people and screeners between humankind and Himself. He could have set up shop in the synagogue and taught about God's laws from behind a pristine pulpit. Peter might have been head of security and would have made sure that no one got anywhere near the hem of His garment. (Ouch, I may have stepped on a toe or three there. Remember, I love you.)

That's not who Jesus was, and that's not how He commanded His followers to behave. Jesus loves people, and while He was on earth, He wanted to be around the people He loved—the people with messed-up lives for which he had the answers. He made a special effort to go where they were. He has instructed us to do the same. Our marching orders are found in Matthew 28:

> Jesus came and told his disciples, "I have been given all authority in heaven and on earth. Therefore, **go** and make disciples of all the nations, baptizing them in the name of the Father and the Son and the Holy Spirit. Teach these new disciples to obey all the commands I have given you. And be sure of this: I am with you always, even to the end of the age." (vv. 18–20, NLT, emphasis mine)

Mutual Solution

The church has a problem because it isn't growing, and in fact, young adults raised in a church continue to drop out at alarming rates. The church isn't growing because it isn't seen as relevant in meeting any actual needs. People attending churches have a problem if they are not fulfilling the call of God on their lives. People will never be content and have authentic joy and fulfillment if they are not doing what God designed and called them to do. They may see God at work more outside of the church than inside, and they want to be a part of what He is doing.

The God solution to the church's growth issue and the attendees' discontentment problem is the same for both. The church needs a structure where people can succeed in their giftings and abilities by meeting the needs of others. People need to be able to engage their faith in a way that tangibly connects to their everyday lives. This will, in turn, bring more people into the church. Our churches will be growing because people will be accomplishing what God designed for them to do. The answer to both groups is related to helping the other succeed.

The following allegory has often been attributed to Rabbi Halm of Romshishok and has found its way into the folklore of many cultures.[6] In any version, one truth from this story is that our success and happiness is rooted in serving others.

One day a man said to God, "God, I would like to know what Heaven and Hell are like."

God showed the man two doors. Inside the first one, in the middle of the room, was a large round table with a

---

6   "Heaven and Hell: The Parable of the Long Spoons," told by Sofo Archon, accessed May 17, 2022, https://sofoarchon.com/heaven-and-hell-the-parable-of-the-long-spoons/.

The Outreaching Church

large pot of vegetable stew. It smelled delicious and made the man's mouth water, but the people sitting around the table were thin and sickly. They appeared to be famished. They were holding spoons with very long handles, and each found it possible to reach into the pot of stew and take a spoonful, but because the handle was longer than their arms, they could not get the spoons back into their mouths.

The man shuddered at the sight of their misery and suffering. God said, "You have seen Hell."

Behind the second door, the room appeared exactly the same. There was a large round table with the large pot of wonderful vegetable stew that made the man's mouth water. The people had the same long-handled spoons, but they were well nourished and plump, laughing and talking.

The man said, "I don't understand."

God smiled. "It is simple," he said. "Love only requires one skill. These people learned early on to share and feed one another, while the greedy only think of themselves."

Reflection Questions

1. Did you identify with the Z's, Millennials, or the Dones in their perceptions of the church and its lack of community impact? If yes how so?
2. Have you ever found yourself frustrated or unable to live out your faith in a way that tangibly impacts those in your community? What did you do as a result? If you are currently involved in ministering to your community, what does that look like?
3. Reflect on the allegory of the long spoons. What are your thoughts regarding how the principle of helping each other relates to your faith community as well as those outside of the family of God?

Chapter 3: Who Is in the House?

One of my favorite questions to ask pastors and church leaders is, "Tell me about the outreach ministries at your church." I define outreach ministries as ministries that are specifically designed to function outside the church to impact and serve the needs of the pre-saved community and ultimately lead them to Christ. The answers generally vary from a puzzled look and an awkward shrug (indicating they don't have any community outreach ministries) to a slightly more confident response about a particular person who attends their church who has a jail or other ministry. If there are established ministries, usually there is a combination of answers indicating the ministries were started accidentally or that an individual had started the outreach and then later began attending the church, bringing it with him or her.

Either way, it seems most churches are unfamiliar with the idea of purposely taking ministries directly into their communities. Many seem stuck in the centuries-old concept of doing one thing to build a church, which is to hold a service with the naive hope that someday someone new might inadvertently wander in. Understand that I'm not against having a service. The writer of Hebrews reminds us, "And let us consider how we may spur one another on toward love and good deeds, not giving up meeting together, as some are in the habit of doing, but encouraging one another—and all the more as you see the Day approaching" (Hebrews 10:24–25, NIV).

The gathering of the saints for encouragement and teaching is of utmost importance. The challenge that most churches face is that they effectively use only a handful of people's gifts and talents, leaving a large majority sitting on the sidelines as spectators, frustrated with their untapped potential. I am advocating there may be additional ways to involve other people besides the pastor to populate the church and, ultimately, heaven.

Is there more we can do than holding a church service once or twice a week and praying that someone will stumble in? If services work to bring people into the Kingdom, let's do them, but if there are additional ways to grow our churches and involve a lot more people in doing so, could we also be open to considering them?

Much of my focus is about church leaders and pastors building an infrastructure for growing outreach ministries and impacting their communities. That said, I understand there are those who are not in leadership positions but are passionate about fulfilling the call of God on their lives and impacting others for Jesus. If you are reading this and find yourself in the second category, I have a few suggestions, and I will be pretty blunt. Some churches may not be in a position to implement these strategies, for whatever reason, but that doesn't absolve you from answering for what God has called you to do. He's given you talents, and he's given you a heart for people. What are you doing with them?

I would advocate that you pray for God's wisdom on how best to use the information in these chapters. Maybe that means giving this book to your pastor or others in leadership and starting a conversation about it. Perhaps it means looking in your community for organizations working in an area that you are passionate about and gifted in. For instance, if you have a heart for unwed mothers, is there a pregnancy crisis center in your area that you could volunteer at? If your compassion is for the incarcerated, is there a jail ministry you could be a part of? Perhaps you love elderly people, and you can serve meals at a senior center or participate in related transportation services.

You get the idea. I will be talking about small groups, but if your church doesn't have a small group structure, that doesn't mean that you can't start one. You can use the strategies in the following few chapters to help you start brainstorming about how to build your team.

To some, especially in church leadership, the idea of developing outreach ministries can seem overwhelming and maybe even scary. Perhaps it sounds like one more thing to do, and your calendar is already covered with obligations. I completely understand, and I want to show you a step-by-step, safe, and easy process to move in a healthy direction that will influence the people outside your church walls for Christ. The result is a game-changer of growth for your church and the Kingdom of God. Your dedication to serving individuals through outreach ministries will be warmly welcomed and appreciated by your congregation and community.

You are most likely already doing many things needed to build outreach ministries; you simply need to change the focus to impact your community more effectively. Many churches are much closer than they realize to having active outreach ministries, and they are greatly relieved when the curtain is pulled back to reveal the minor changes that need to be made to effectively impact their city for Jesus. There are no quick fixes, just steady refinements that will result in healthy ministries changing lives now and for eternity. If you are reading this book because you are ready to get in the game, but you aren't sure how to best use your skills for Kingdom growth, stick with me! It's easier than you think.

Start with the Solution

In his business book *How to Attain Financial Security and Self Confidence*, author Marvin Small popularized the saying, "Find a need and fill it"[7] as the key to lasting success. Earlier, we discussed Robert H. Schuller's expanded version of this saying. This is a true statement; however, the text has

---
[7] Marvin Small, *How to Attain Financial Security and Self Confidence* (New York: Simon and Schuster, 1953).

The Outreaching Church

an underlying assumption that you have the wherewithal to solve the need. When a person needs a glass of water, you can give him one . . . as long as you have the glass of water. If someone needs a ride to a doctor's appointment, you can provide one, as long as you have a driver's license and a car. However, solving current societal needs can be much more complicated. There are many issues that we may not have the specific knowledge or ability to resolve.

Think of the people in our communities who need extra help: the incarcerated, families of the incarcerated, the homeless, victims of sex trafficking, and the elderly. Also, people with special needs, depression, addictions, financial hardships, sexual identity questions, marital problems, teenager issues, educational deficiencies, mental health hardships, and the list goes on and on. Some of these matters are very complicated and may require advanced specialization or knowledge to effect change. Most of these issues are very large, and layers of problems affect these demographics. For example, do homeless people only have the problem of not having a home, or is there a gamut of related concerns affecting them that have resulted in homelessness? It is a copout, a cheap easy answer to say people just need Jesus, when we are not willing to get out of our churches and be involved

> It is a copout, a cheap easy answer to say people just need Jesus, when we are not willing to get out of our churches and be involved with their lives, showing them solutions that lead them to Jesus.

with their lives, showing them solutions that lead them to Jesus. That is real love.

Knowing there is a problem or need is essential; however, I recommend starting **with the answer**. Start identifying the solutions you already have by recognizing the abilities God has placed in the people in your church. There is no shortage of problems to solve, but there is a shortage of capable, talented, willing people to solve them. If you start with people's giftings, you will discover **God has given us the answers** to people's dilemmas. It's beautiful and eternity-changing when we see God moving through His people to answer the world's problems.

The idea of starting with the answer rather than the problem can seem convoluted, so let's talk about it more. This is where you who are discontent and gifted of God come in. You know you have a passion for certain people in society or you have abilities you know would be beneficial to others. You are God's answer to someone's prayers. Let's find out more.

Several years ago, when I was preparing a sermon for a local church, I had a revelation about the Parable of the Talents in Matthew 25. That God encounter led me to write my book, *Well Done: Finding and Fulfilling God's Plan for Your Life*. Without rewriting the entire thing, let me give you a quick recap of what the Holy Spirit revealed to me about this story.

The Outreaching Church

In this parable, the Master gave a varying number of talents to his three servants; then, he took off on a long journey. He expected that those talents would be put to work for an increase. When he returned, he found that two of the servants had done just that. They had invested his talents and gained a return. His response was, "Well done, good and faithful servant! You have been faithful with a few things; I will put you in charge of many things. Come and share your master's happiness!" (Matthew 25:23, NIV). The third servant, however, due to fear, laziness, or some other lame excuse, hid the talent and did nothing with it. Let's just say the Master's response was less than enthusiastic, and there may have been something about "utter darkness" and "weeping and gnashing of teeth." Wouldn't want to be that guy!

While many interpret (and rightly so) that talents in this parable equate to a sum of money, they can also refer to natural skills, abilities, and things of value. The New Testament talks about the gifts that have been given to us by God for building up His Kingdom and His church. Our takeaway from this story should be that we have each been gifted by God, and we are going to be held accountable for how we discover, use, and increase those talents. I'm sure none of us want to hear, "You wicked and lazy servant" at the end of our life. Let's contend to hear, "Well done!"

I can't think of a better place to use the gifts and abilities that God has given me than to release people made in His image out of their bondages and introduce them to Him. Using the skills God has given us for the people He called us to is a fantastic return on what has been entrusted to us. When we use our combined talents, we have the answers to the world's problems. As Paul wrote to the church at Ephesus, "For we are His workmanship, created in Christ Jesus for good works, which God prepared beforehand that we should walk in them" (Ephesians 2:10, NKJV).

If we take our eyes off ourselves, listen to the Holy Spirit, and serve others with the solutions He has placed inside of us, the answers will work, and people's lives will be transformed. As their lives are changing, we will also have the opportunity to lead them into an eternity-altering relationship with Jesus. There is nothing better! Yes, the world is incredibly messed up, but the great news is we are pre-wired with God's solutions that will ultimately bring them freedom and to Jesus.

Look Around

To begin this process, I suggest the leadership take a mental inventory of who is in their congregation. This is all you who are faithfully attending and sitting unrecognized in our churches every week. We as leaders should think, "Are there currently mature Christians in our congregation who have an ability or passion for helping those in need, or who already work with a particular segment of society outside our church walls? Would these people like to use those same attributes to serve and influence people for Christ?"

The Outreaching Church

When I ask these questions, many pastors immediately default with the answer, "I can't think of anybody." In that case, we could ask some follow-up questions:

- Do you know anyone with a heart for people incarcerated in jails or prisons?
- How about individuals who are interested in the homeless or downtrodden?
- How about the elderly or people with special needs?
- Do you know anyone who has a background in business or who likes to network with other businesspeople?
- Do you know anyone who had a tough time as a teenager and wants to help other teens?
- Do you know people with building or mechanical abilities?
- Do you know anyone who likes to work on cars?
- How about helping single moms balance their life?

If you are reading this book because you are looking for a way to impact your community for Christ, do these questions stir something in you? All these activities and so many more are possible outreach ministries.

When I ask these questions, there may be more recognition and awareness of individuals with abilities. However, if pastors say they don't know of anyone who has some of these talents, unfortunately, it shows they are disconnected from their people. They don't understand how the Father has wired and gifted those they lead.

It could be that there is a culture where pastors or their congregation don't think they can do anything connected to God except by being a pastor, so they have stifled their compassion for helping others. We can change this culture; it's just a longer route. Our Father has placed His remarkable heart of understanding and abilities within our congregations as a clue to the problems they are called to help solve. Do you think people have this incredible compassion and insight to help specific groups of people for no reason? Of course not! The pertinent question is, how do we take a mature Christian with a tender heart for a segment of society and create an opportunity for ministry to happen?

If you don't have a system for identifying people's gifts and passions, I suggest you start there. This foundation is vital to the success of any long-term ministry. The *Well Done* book is one place to begin, and there are multiple resources and inventories available to help people understand their motivational giftings and how to develop them.

Observer or Leader?

Let's look at Ephesians 4 for continued insights into how we should function as a church. In this portion of Paul's letter to the church at Ephesus, he lays out the job description for church leadership. Paul writes, "Now these are the gifts Christ gave to the church: the apostles, the prophets, the evangelists, and the pastors and teachers. Their responsibility is to *equip God's people to do his work* and build up the church, the body of Christ" (Ephesians 4:11–12, NLT, emphasis mine). A huge barrier to developing outreach ministries is a church model in which the pastor does all the work, and the congregation is full of passive observers. In this framework, outreach ministries are just one more thing for the pastor to spearhead. The problem with that model is it is not what the Bible teaches.

Our job description as leaders is to *equip* the saints (our congregations) *for the work* of the ministry (meeting people's needs). The great news is these people are already pre-wired with the abilities or talents of God for their success. Our people already have the interior wiring, desire, and giftings to help people. They can identify what God has placed in their hearts because they have a passion, compassion, or an innate desire to help in these areas. So, the first step is to assist your people in identifying their calling if they haven't already.

Next, it is our responsibility as leaders to **provide a functioning culture** and structure where our people can be the answer to other people's prayers. If you are not sure how to establish this culture, you may want to review *The Connected Church* and *The Empowered Church* books. Applying the combined knowledge from these resources equals an empowered connected church that is outreaching and changing our communities for Christ.

Cultivating Culture

A key element for success is to develop a culture where people are encouraged to identify what God would have them do. It is the leadership's responsibility to create a healthy environment where people know they are responsible for growing and moving forward to accomplish what God has placed on their hearts. In this kind of healthy, empowered environment, individual and ministry growth happens.

If I have a handful of various grains, I probably couldn't tell you which seed will grow up to be which plant. However, if I plant those seeds in rich, moist soil with plenty of warmth, water, and sunlight, it is easy for me to identify the plants as they are growing. Many sprouts may look the same when they are just coming up, but if I can keep them developing, it will soon be evident what kind of plant it is. When I'm looking at a six-foot corn stalk, it is easy to identify, "Yep, no doubt about it, that is corn. That shorter grassy looking one is wheat." I can identify them, and I'm not even a geographer, or is that a biographer? Oops, maybe a botanist? Anyway, it's the same with people. If we put people in a healthy environment to grow, their giftings will also become apparent.

In reality, it does get a little more complicated because no two people or callings are precisely alike. In fact, no two of anything are 100% alike. Just because a person is called to a particular ministry, it will not look exactly like any other ministry. Think about it in the natural world. There are reportedly over 1,000 different types of bananas. Wow! Is that a mindblower or what? I just wanted bananas with my peanut butter, and now I have over 1,000 different choices. That's not all. Of the 1,000 different types of bananas, no two individual ones are identical. God, you are so amazing!

Many people may think because they are called to a specific ministry, it should be like someone else's. That may or may not be the case. While it's essential to learn from others, especially those more seasoned in an area we feel called to serve in, we need to get over the dead-end thought process of being identical. Let's strive to become the best version of who God created us to be. Let's create a culture where people identify what they are designed for and make strides to multiply their talents invested in Kingdom work.

The Ultimate of All Success

When we have a supportive culture, people can move forward, discover their giftings, and fulfill God's plan for their life. Those who want to progress need to know there is a path to accomplish what God has wired them for. One of the best ways to create this environment is through encouraging sermons and leadership development that urges people to go after the ultimate of all success. According to the Parable of the Talents, the goal of our lives is to hear, "Well done, thou good and faithful servant." Is there anything you would rather accomplish with your life? The number-one attribute for success is to create a healthy culture where people are encouraged to hear "well done" from Jesus as the culmination of their life's work.

> The number-one attribute for success is to create a healthy culture where people are encouraged to hear "well done" from Jesus as the culmination of their life's work.

Wouldn't it be great if everyone in your congregation was continually inspired to succeed for the Kingdom? When they are seeking to hear "well done" from Jesus, you will not have to coerce them to step up and volunteer, attend church, tithe, or pray. They will naturally take the initiative to succeed for the Kingdom and your church. These desires become the motivation for them to serve a segment of society. In the next chapter, let's look at a straightforward structure that can lead you to start many successful outreach ministries from a basic foundational building block.

The Outreaching Church

Reflection Questions

1. If you are a church leader/pastor, what is your experience with outreach ministries? Do you have functioning ministries that are impacting your pre-saved communities, or is this an area of struggle? What have you tried? Has it been as successful as you had hoped?
2. If you are not in ministry as your profession, what has your experience been with outreach ministries? Have you been involved with outreaches in your church or other organizations? How has that gone?
3. Does your church have a process to help people identify their giftings and the call of God on their lives? If so, is it effective and what are you doing with that information? If not, how can you start taking steps to develop this process, or identify these giftings in your own life?
4. Reflect on Ephesians 4. If you are in church leadership, how are you equipping the saints for the work of the ministry, or are you doing it all yourself? How can you do more equipping so the church body can carry the ministry forward? As an individual, what part are you playing in the work of the ministry?

Chapter 4: Structured for Success

There are multiple analogies in the Bible, especially the in the New Testament, about connection. Jesus talks about being grafted into the vine in John 15:1–6 so that we can bear fruit. What we ultimately produce is related to our relationship with Him, and if we are cut off from the vine, we cannot produce what we were designed for. The church is the bride of Christ (see Revelation 19:7–9 and Ephesians 5:25–32), the ultimate of all connections, and in other portions of scripture, we are described as individual parts, connected to form a functioning body with Jesus as the head (see 1 Corinthians 12:12–31 and Ephesians 4:11–16).

All these references make clear that connection is vital to fulfilling our purpose here on earth. We must be connected to Christ, and we must be joined to one another as a body of believers in order to succeed. If a vine is going to be healthy and grow, producing rich, heavy fruit, it needs a trellis to attach to, giving it stability and allowing it to flourish. When a vine is cut off from its support system, it will eventually wither and die. Let's talk about a basic structure so flexible that many different healthy vines of outreach ministries can be developed from it.

The Outreaching Church

Creating Community

Part of the challenge for us in our modern-day culture is to connect with people effectively. In this historic time, people are more connected at a surface level through social media than previous generations, but far more disconnected from deep, meaningful relationships. Gone (for most people) are the days of the multigenerational family farm, neighborhood barn raisings, and the natural community that existed even as recently as 60 or 70 years ago.

God designed us to be connected and involved with others. Unfortunately, because of our incredible mobility, fractured family relationships, the ability to work remotely, and many other factors related to modern society, more people are disconnected from authentic, healthy relationships than ever before. Being disconnected from meaningful relationships leads to a host of issues. If we are ever going to fulfill God's calling on our lives, we must reestablish these connections.

A great way to foster relationships is through some sort of small group. The term "small groups" can be polarizing, and many of us may have had a variety of experiences with small group concepts. Small groups are like anything else; they are what you make them. I tell our leaders that in tough times, people will get connected to small groups because they are seeking relationships and answers for their life. Either they will default to a small group at the local bar during happy hour, or they will connect to one of the small groups through our church. Which one could save their marriage and their family?

Many churches have tried small groups with mixed outcomes. Some churches have had dismal results, and on the other end of the spectrum are many large churches with excellent results. Small groups are a necessary infrastructural building block in developing a healthy, growing church.

As congregations grow, it is a challenge for a pastor to have a personal relationship with everyone, yet relationships are vital to holding people in and creating a discipleship pathway. Even with additional pastors, there still needs to be a framework where people can build personal relationships with each other.

Small groups create a wonderful place where relationships deepen and serve as a net to hold people in and connect them to others around a common curriculum or interest. If people have personal or health problems, it creates a natural support system of others who care, pray, and follow up with them. We have had small groups follow up with individuals by delivering food or visiting them in the hospital.

Discipleship is also a huge advantage of small groups, especially when using a solid curriculum that will help people mature in their walk with Christ. People can discover their giftings and set about putting them to use. Small groups can help in this maturation process and connect people together who have similar passions and skills.

Our church's goal is to connect as many people as possible to healthy relationships through our small group structure. I know people can receive substantially more godly wisdom and encouragement in our small groups than the general attendees at the local bar. I regularly hear positive stories of individuals impacted by the association of small groups. I know these are only a small fraction of the overwhelmingly positive results occurring. I'm sure there are thousands of life-giving interactions through our small groups: prayers for marriages, children, families, jobs, health, finances. Small groups give the potential for personal connection that is hard to create in a large church service.

The power of small groups is amazing, and we can utilize them to establish connections and outreach ministries. We have a saying that we want to build our church larger and smaller simultaneously. Smaller from the standpoint of more small groups, which are the relational building blocks on which a larger number of attending people can be connected.

Programs . . . or Not

Some churches may look at large events to draw new people in as a means to build their congregation or reach their community. I'm not a big event or program proponent, especially without a well-defined outcome or purpose.

Large events can take substantial manpower and resources, and if there is not an effective, on-purpose follow-up, we can do a lot of work for very little Kingdom return. Instead, I prefer ongoing repetitive ministry through small groups. Small groups may not be flashy, but they work. We have all seen individuals who, in the moment, are impacted at large crusades or programs. But if they are not quickly connected into a local group of believers, they can soon fall back into old habits and relationships resulting in them never being seen again.

When people accept Jesus, they are fully inflated with God's life-changing possibilities. However, like a balloon, they also have a very slow leak, and without intentional input, they gradually deflate spiritually as they wander back into their previous associations and lifestyle. The key for new believers to remain healthy and build on the momentum created by the event is to continue checking their spiritual tank. New believers can get refilled when they connect with other life-giving believers through small groups, serving teams, or church services so they can continue the process of renewing their minds to strengthen the new creation they are in Christ. The power of positive association is huge for new believers who may or may not have any saved friends or church background. Large outreaches can work if there is a comprehensive follow-up plan that includes connecting people to small groups.

The Outreaching Church

Game Changer

As noted earlier, many churches struggle with developing and running small groups. Perhaps they were relying on the "BIG EVENT" to spur church growth and that didn't work, so now they are trying something new. Church leaders may hear that small groups are the key to church growth, so they start without really buying in and understanding what they are doing or what it takes to make these groups successful. Let's talk about a few keys to making small groups work, because I believe they are essential for growth and discipleship.

The most crucial component for the success of anything is the leader, and this includes developing small groups at your church. Putting a competent leader in charge who understands and believes in their potential is essential.

The second key to small group success is developing a culture that supports small groups. For small groups to succeed, it is imperative that the senior pastor believes in them and regularly talks about their importance. We encourage all staff members to lead a small group at our church. If the senior pastor is leading a small group and all the staff are leading small groups and small groups are being talked about routinely from the pulpit, it clearly conveys that these are important to our church and culture and should be important to the congregation.

It is a proven principle that what we talk about, we get more of. If you want small groups to be successful, they must be talked about and referred to all the time. I spoke to one very large church where small groups were thriving. I asked how often they talked about small groups from the pulpit. Their answer? Every week.

From a growth perspective, we use the basic foundational structure of small groups as a framework for our serving teams, traditional small groups, and outreach ministries. This fundamental concept is a game-changer for how we see and build small groups and the results they produce.

Generally speaking, people can sign up and start participating in most small groups or outreach ministries at any time. While some groups have a specific curriculum with a definitive time frame, we encourage most of our groups to operate year-round and welcome new members at any time. At the time of writing this book, our church publishes a printed directory of all our small groups with contact information for the leader and any other pertinent data. The directory is available on our church website.

In addition, we hold three specific small group expos each year. Expos are where people can get information and sign up for a small group. We schedule one after the first of the year, one in the summer, and one in the fall. We usually have the expo after each service in a very visible area like our lobby, where people can meet the leaders, ask questions, and sign up. The expos take place on two consecutive weeks for maximum exposure.

Our church also provides signups virtually on our website. As you get more groups, you will need to move the information to a website with search parameters because it isn't feasible to list all the groups in a directory or have all of them represented at an expo. But you can still introduce and promote the newest small groups at the expo.

Free-Market Groups

Small groups can be called by various names: community groups, cell groups, life groups, or home groups. Even though small groups may not technically be referred to as outreach ministries, it is a **huge mistake** not to treat them as such. There are many types, styles, and approaches to building these small groups in ways that can influence and serve people in our communities. We refer to the type of small groups we develop at Life Church as free-market small groups.

Free-market small groups are based on the concept of free markets in the business world, as related to the free enterprise system. These small groups are market-driven, which means our small group leaders have the flexibility to start groups on subjects that they feel would serve the market (community). These groups can take place almost anywhere and at any time, on virtually any topic that is not contrary to the Bible or to our church culture. They are all based on what the leader is gifted and able to facilitate and what the people they are serving would be interested in attending.

There is substantial flexibility in the type of groups leaders can develop under this model. In essence, free-market small groups are driven by the "consumer," meaning they succeed if they are what people want, need, and are willing to participate in. If we serve the people who attend our small groups and provide value, they will keep showing up and possibly invite others. If we don't give attendees value, which means meeting a need, they won't attend the group. When people don't show up, it indicates to the leader that in some way, they did not serve their people well. Once again, the good news is the leader can change or try something else to better meet people's needs. Isn't this the way it works in business? If businesses don't provide a quality service to meet the needs of the public, they adapt to serve people better or go out of business.

Let's take a moment and ponder what developing free-market small groups can produce. As people step into this leadership role, they discover their gifts and abilities, as well as the passions that God has placed in them. They also experience God moving through them to impact the lives of others. The leaders are getting real-time feedback on how well they are utilizing those abilities to serve others. If the groups have positive results, that's fantastic. If the results are not as good as hoped for, changes can be made to more effectively impact lives. These small groups create the opportunity for ministry to happen on a variety of levels.

The Outreaching Church

Small Group Foundation

There are several ways to move people forward in ministry, and one of the best ways is to use small groups as the primary building blocks for flourishing outreach ministries. Let's look at how this happens. Small groups are a flexible structure for developing an incubator effect in which baby outreach ministries can be started and mature. It is also a safe way for leadership to move their gifted people forward (and influence their community) outside of the church walls for the Kingdom of God.

A huge key in starting outreach ministries is to start small. Don't try to begin 10 ministries at once or even have one massive outreach the first time around. There are too many pitfalls and unknown variables. As we will discuss, the best way I have found to launch an outreach is through the infrastructure of a small group.

Start with one or two dependable believers with skill and ability in a specific area of service and move them forward as leaders. Then work out the process as you progress. This will be your opportunity to take a mature person through the trailblazing process that others will follow by moving a small group to an outreach ministry. You will learn many great things through the development phases, so enjoy the journey and refine it for others who will be following later.

My viewpoint is that I only build ministries based on a quality leader. **Do not start a ministry based solely on a**

need. There has to be a solid leader who is gifted with a solution and passion about the cause, or we don't move forward. As John Maxwell says, "Everything rises and falls on leadership,"[8] so don't proceed without a high-quality leader. Trying to build a ministry or organization without a gifted person at the helm is very painful and destined to fail. There has never been a single, great, lasting organization with terrible leadership; it is an impossibility.

Small Beginnings

What worldwide Christian leader grew up being sexually abused by her alcoholic father, was cheated on by her first husband, and stole regularly? That doesn't sound like a great start to an internationally recognized ministry. The leader of this substantial outreach that has touched millions of lives also admits to being terrible at speaking and having a very controlling attitude toward people in her early years of ministry. So what happened?

I'm sure many things changed, but one of the critical things was that she started an early morning Bible class at a cafeteria. After joining a small interdenominational church, she taught a weekly women's Bible study in her home for the next five years. Eventually, she was invited to lead a Bible study at her church, which she viewed as her introduction to public speaking. Over several years, this little

---

8 John Maxwell, *The 21 Irrefutable Laws of Leadership: Follow Them and People Will Follow You* (Nashville, TN: HarperChristian Resources, 2007).

The Outreaching Church

Bible study grew in attendance to over 500 women every Thursday morning.[9]

God developed Joyce Meyer over the years of her faithful service in leading small groups. How many Christian leaders have you heard about who began in ministry in a similar fashion? The answer is . . . A LOT. International ministries are not born overnight. Rarely, if ever, does someone get a call to speak in front of a coliseum full of people without having proven themselves on a much smaller scale first. Regardless of how big a ministry is called to grow, small groups are a safe place to start from. They allow us to mature in interacting with people, developing our skill sets, growing in our knowledge of the Bible, and presenting God's Word effectively.

---

9   Bill Smith and Carolyn Tuft, "Meyer Traces Her Fervor to Early Abuse, Alcohol," *St. Louis Post-Dispatch*, November 15, 2003, https://web.archive.org/web/20060127003333/http://www.stltoday.com/stltoday/news/special/joycemeyer.nsf/0/1D29266A7F855B2886256DDF-00701F8A?OpenDocument; Joyce Meyer, *Healing the Soul of a Woman* (Nashville, TN: FaithWords, 2018), 49.

Reflection Questions

1. What is in place at your church to foster relationships? How is it working?
2. If someone new comes to your fellowship, how do they connect with others? How do you follow up with new believers in order to disciple them and keep them connected?
3. If you have small groups at your church, are they flourishing? Are they primarily serving those in your congregation, or do they have an outward focus? What refinements could you make in this area? What are your reflections on the idea of free-market small groups?
4. Start identifying potential leaders in your congregation. How can you equip and empower them in the area of outreach ministry?

Chapter 5: What Is in Your Hand?

After describing to Moses His grand plan for freeing the Israelite slaves in Exodus 3, God ran into some pushback from His chosen leader. Moses spent several verses explaining to God why he (Moses) was the wrong guy for the job. Then, in Exodus 4:2, God asks Moses a pivotal question, "What is that in your hand?" (NIV). Since He is God, I'm assuming He already knew Moses had a staff in his hand. I believe God was trying to bring Moses' attention to what he already possessed—his staff. God indicated by his answer that Moses' staff could be used as the answer to the Israelites' prayers. What if Moses had said, "I have a dirt clod"? God could have said, "Yep, that will work." God could have used anything in Moses' hand to set the people free. The issue wasn't what he held.

What if Moses had said that he was a plumber or a mechanic, or that he was great at making bricks? God may have said, "Whatever you have and dedicate for My use will work." It doesn't matter what it is; it can still get the job done. It doesn't make any difference what is in our hands; it's *Who* is working through what is in our hands that is important. No matter what we have, even if it's just a stick, a slingshot, or some empty jars and a little bit of olive oil, when God is part of the solution, giants fall, miracles happen, and lives are changed.

What's in your hand? What talents, abilities, or gifts can you devote to God? When you dedicate them to God, lives change, and people are released from years of bondage. We can follow in the footsteps of legendary men and women of God and commit what we have to the Lord and watch great things happen.

When we develop our gifts and abilities, they are a staff in our hands that can be used to influence people for Christ. Let's hear from an amazing couple using their staff to impact many lives for the Kingdom. Stefani is certified to use horses to help people with mental afflictions, and Monty is gifted in many ways to influence those around him for Christ. The name of their innovative outreach is God and Horses.

We utilize our abilities and background of working with horses to offer trauma-focused equine-assisted services, therapy, and ministry to those suffering from trauma and abuse. We use scripture and science to facilitate reorganizing the brain and rebuilding neural pathways that are lost in trauma.

We serve domestic violence victims, abused children, veterans, individuals with drug addiction, people with relationship issues, and anyone who has problems coping. Over the last three years, we have worked with over 200 people. We have helped a lady experience freedom after 55 years of oppression. It was beautiful to see her entire countenance and body change as she was released from this extended bondage.

We've had numerous healings, including seeing children set free from abuse and its effects. We currently have clients diagnosed with schizophrenia and borderline personality disorder who are experiencing life-changing results. We have also seen marriages restored. Everywhere we go, people ask why we have eight horses, and it allows us to talk about Jesus and what we do with God and Horses.

We are very thankful that we could start God and Horses as a small group before becoming an outreach ministry. Starting as a small group enabled us to recruit a team of people and develop our approach to ministry. The guidance and support we received from our church's leadership were pivotal to our success. Now we also do ministry in another state and take members of our team with us to minister at a domestic violence center in a rural community. It has been a blessing to attend numerous outreach trainings that further enable us to impact our community and effectively develop our team. During these critical times, it is vital that we are equipped to go and reach those who can't or won't come to a church, but still need to hear the gospel.

That is a powerful story of how lives are changed because of cultivated and developed abilities. Use the following list to get your creative juices flowing regarding how to dedicate your abilities to Kingdom use. You may have talents you don't recognize. Don't take them for granted! We cannot do anything without the grace of God. You have those abilities because of God's grace, so don't discount them. Celebrate them! These gifts are the answer to someone else's needs.

Mechanical	Constitution Class
Appliance Repair	Child Care
Car Repair	Home Schooling
Construction	Cleaning
Remodeling	Cooking
Welding	Organization
Woodworking	Decorating
Songwriting	Gardening
Singing	Debt Reduction
Education	Investing
Tutoring	Estate Planning
Interview Skills	Photography
Résumé Prep	Video Production
Counseling	Social Media
Addiction Recovery	Graphic Design
Grief	Politics
Real Estate	Sports
Parenting	Hobbies

This is only a very small list. Pray about it. God has given you talents and abilities that you can use for Kingdom increase. You can experience amazing fulfillment when you put your abilities to work to positively change the lives of others.

The Outreaching Church

Whatever you excel at can be a staff God has placed in your hand.

Outreach Made Easy Peasy

Do people in our congregation need help with their marriage? That answer would be yes. What about the people in our communities? That answer is also yes. Are there people in our congregations who have a good marriage and want to encourage others to have the same? Probably another yes. Could these people lead small groups that are focused on helping marriages succeed? Once again, that answer should be yes. Is there godly wisdom from the Bible that would be a huge part of having a healthy marriage? I think we are on a roll with another yes.

We now have (almost) effortlessly established a small group based on the giftings of our people that can serve our congregation as well as couples in our community. We have, in effect, birthed an outreach ministry (with very few labor pains)! A side benefit is that the pastor doesn't need to do all of the marriage counseling. Wouldn't that be a trifecta of amazing accomplishments!

What if we built multiple, successful marriage small groups focused on strengthening the family unit, improving communication skills, and modeling relationships on biblical values? What if instead of in-crisis couples doing months of one-on-one counseling, these hurting partners were encouraged to attend a marriage small group led by mature believers? Not only could they receive godly counsel, but they would also be surrounded and encouraged by other fruitful couples. That sounds like a huge win for everyone. Your church could even be known in your community as the place to go to for great help with your marriage!

Marriage is just one of a host of areas that we, as the body of Christ, are gifted and passionate to help with. Starting need-meeting small groups effectively strengthens our congregation and can reach out to serve our community. Do people need help with finances, raising kids, or even cooking skills? Do people need help with recovering from grief? How about couples seeking premarital counseling? You get the idea. How easy is that?

Let's Help People

How many groups could we start with the similar application of meeting the needs of our congregation and community using the talents and abilities that God gifted to his people? It could seem endless. These groups are designed around quality content with the goal of helping people. They create conversation and interaction, leading to healthy biblical answers and nurturing relationships. Creating an environment where we can share someone's burden is a gigantic win. People need to know we care about them and are praying for them. This is powerful! But it gets better because we can actually help people with the wisdom of the Bible.

The Outreaching Church

There are close to a zillion curriculums available for these groups. Well, maybe not a zillion, but at least a large number of ready-to-use, proven materials. Below are just a few of the main need-meeting groups that we can establish to help our congregation and people in our communities.

Finances: Financial Peace University, Crown Financial

Divorce recovery: Divorce Care

People going through depression and grief: Grief Share

Marriage problems: Marriage Mentors, Focus on the Family, Marriage Encounter

Addictions: Celebrate Recovery

Now that I've got you all hyped up to start at least a dozen small group/outreach ministries tomorrow at the very latest . . . let's return to my very first admonition. **We start with a seasoned competent leader** who has a gift, talent, or ability in a given area. We identify those they have the compassion to help, which creates the opportunity for them to be someone's life-changing answer through the vehicle of a small group.

> The equation for success is:
> Individuals Ability x Passion or Compassion + Small Group = Jesus's Answer

The equation for success is:

Individuals Ability x Passion or Compassion + Small Group = Jesus's Answer

Possibilities

We care about the elderly. We start a group that provides rides to church, runs errands, or accompanies the elderly to doctor visits. We partner with local nursing homes to provide companionship.

We care about the dying. We interact as hospice or provide respite care.

We have a building/mechanical skill set. We build ramps for wheelchair-bound veterans or bunk beds for low-income children.

We have an automotive skill set. We repair cars for single moms or restore cars to give to low-income families.

We care about the homeless. We provide breakfast in the park, take water bottles out on hot days, knit hats and scarves for cold weather.

We have a cooking skill. We provide meals for new moms and those recovering from surgery, share meals with widows or widowers, partner with a homeless or shelter ministry.

We have computer tech skills. We help shut-ins, the medically challenged, or the elderly so they can watch services online or attend virtual small groups.

We have athletic abilities. We start an after-school program and coach and mentor young people. We form a team and compete locally. We form an accountability group for those working at developing a healthier lifestyle.

We have business skills. We build felony-friendly work environments, work-study and job training programs for youth, financial or business education to help start-ups.

We have a teaching gift. We tutor students, help with GEDs and résumé prep, and teach English to refugees.

Again, these are just a few examples to get your own ideas flowing. There are SO many possibilities when God's giftings and compassion come together in His people to serve others and share the love of Jesus.

Whatever you like to do, you can invite other people to do it with you, and you have just created a small group that can influence people toward God. That's it! Once again, how easy can this be!

The reality is you don't have to be the number-one expert in the world at what you teach because the goal is connecting with others. While we always strive for excellence and we want to continue to grow and develop our abilities, the real focus is on creating connection while meeting a genuine need. This connection is not only for our congregation but also for people in our communities. It becomes a way for us to meet and be part of their life journey. It also gives us the opportunity to impact and change people's lives in a tangible way toward the Kingdom. We can be the answer to someone else's prayers, and the Kingdom gets populated simultaneously.

Start Here

I've mentioned just a few of literally hundreds of areas of possible outreach ministry. While understanding potential needs is vital, as I will continue to shout from the rooftops, the best place to start is with a mature leader who has a gift that serves others. This gifting allows us to connect with others around this function or activity far more easily than trying to fit a leader into a ministry they are neither gifted for nor excited about. If people are not quite seasoned enough to lead an outreach ministry, a small group gives them the opportunity and time to mature.

I like to start with themes people are already interested in or good at. If this is also what they are passionate about, it is a natural place to begin and becomes a gathering point to bring people together. Here are some examples of how this could play out.

We can start a group that enjoys decorating and bring people together around this common interest. To take this ability a step further in impact, we ask the question, is there some practical way we can use the giftings in our group to help others? Does the church need a facelift in some areas? How about the lobby or bathrooms? This group can use their God-given abilities to make the church more attractive.

Do others in the community want to learn this skill or be around other people of common interest? Of course they

The Outreaching Church

do, and they can be part of this group. Are there shut-ins who would love to have their home freshened up? Once again, the answer is yes. Okay, we just became an outreach ministry, entering a shut-in's home to bring decorations and possibly prayer, acceptance, and love. Wasn't that an easy and natural evolution of using our gifts to serve someone else?

These examples could go on for pages. All it takes is a little shift in focus. The great thing is there are people who are already gifted in all these areas in your church, and there are also people who have needs in all these areas both inside and outside of your church. A gifted person can create a group around their area of expertise/interest, people from the community can attend, and all the functions of the group can impact and enrich others' lives. This is a win, win, win.

Reflection Questions

1. As you reflect on your personal giftings, what is in your hand? What talents, abilities, or gifts can you devote to God?
2. In what ways do you think God can use those gifts and abilities to grow His kingdom? Spend some time in prayer on this topic and ask the Holy Spirit for His wisdom.
3. If you are currently attending or leading a small group, what shift in focus could you make that would lead the group in the direction of being an outreach ministry?

Chapter 6: Change Your Focus

Think of the endless gifts God has placed in our congregations. All those abilities are also the answers to someone else's needs and possibly even their prayers. It is great news that God has already gifted people attending your church with solutions to the problems in your community. When we serve others, we are positioned to interact with members of our community and influence them for the Kingdom.

Four Steps in Moving Forward

We have talked about how easy it is to develop outreach ministries. Let's recap the process before we get into more examples of developing these impactful ministries.

#1 Start with a great leader. A quality leader is the key to success. An effective leader can start a group about reading comic books or making mud pies, and everyone will get saved and discipled. That is just what a good leader does. On the other hand, a poor leader can present the book of John, and everyone might denounce God and rob a bank. Okay, perhaps I'm exaggerating, but you get the idea. The leader is the most important factor in the success of the group.

#2 Analyze the risk. We should always consider the risk of starting a small group, outreach ministry, or making any significant decision. Risk is always essential to understand and mitigate. For example, a very mature Christian wants to start a life group to teach people how to throw axes at other people attached to a revolving target. The goal is to throw the ax close to the spinning person but miss them. This group may have a quality leader. (I might be reevaluating my assessment of them at this point.) It could even be a great source of unsaved people accepting Jesus into their hearts as they spin in circles before the axes fly. That said, the risk is probably more than our insurance company (or I) is willing to approve.

On a more serious note, there is a wide array of risks related to ministry that we are always trying to avoid or minimize. Think of all the goofy things people can do with someone else and you can come up with a large list of potential pitfalls. Here are just a few. People might present their personal beliefs over what the Bible says or in opposition to what the pastor is teaching. Gossip or moral failings can also be very destructive. People might use a small group leadership position to promote their business, multi-level marketing, a financial opportunity or investment. Whatever the mind of man can imagine, people may try it. However, if our mantra is to move people forward in positions of leadership slowly, these potential issues can be revealed or caught early on before causing widespread damage or division.

#3 Start slow and small. One of the best ways to mitigate risk is starting slow and prototyping the idea. Again, this is where small groups come in. This method limits risk because it lowers exposure and the number of people we are involved with. It is one thing if we try out an idea on three people and it flops. It's quite another to try an idea for the first time with a coliseum full of people. Small groups not only give the advantage of starting small, but they also provide the added component of time. A small group may continue several years before it is refined enough to become a full-fledged outreach ministry. Time is an excellent vetting process that limits the risk for new ideas. Start small and dream big!

#4 What does God say? Perhaps it should go without saying, but I'll say it anyway. We should be praying and continually seeking God's direction in all our endeavors. What God says is always the trump card; however, have you noticed that God doesn't necessarily weigh in on every decision we are trying to make? That is where we need to continually look at the leader, lower risk through time and exposure, and judge how lives are impacted.

Our ministry to the elderly in assisted care facilities is what we refer to as the Senior Campus Outreach. This outreach is an example of God's compassion to the elderly of our community. Kristie, the outreach leader, knew that God had called her to minister to seniors, but she was also doing many other good things around the church. When she came to the God-inspired revelation that doing the senior ministry was connected to her hearing "well done," Kristie realized this was not just another good thing to be involved in, but it was HER call from God. This is what He had for her to do, and she needed to get with it! To start with, she needed to stop doing good things and focus wholly on the area she was accountable for.

Kristie's Story

Our team goes into senior independent living, assisted living, and nursing homes and provides a church service every Sunday morning. We serve seniors or those with physical or mental limitations. We fellowship with them; develop relationships: and offer friendship, prayer, salvation, and spiritual support to those we serve. This past year we ministered to approximately 135 individuals every week.

We have seen both staff's and residents' lives impacted through this ministry. Three residents with whom we developed relationships passed away last year. When we met, all three were unbelievers but accepted the Lord and grew in their knowledge of His love for them before they died.

One woman I had personally been visiting for over a year and shared the gospel message with received the Lord while on her deathbed. She could not speak, so I asked her to blink her eyes if she would like to make Jesus the Lord of her life. She blinked her eyes over and over. I led her through the prayer and asked her to blink her eyes to show she agreed with the prayer. Praise the Lord! She was born again! We even had a med-tech caregiver give her heart to the Lord recently as she was observing one of our services.

We are affiliating with other outreach ministries for increased impact. The Hand and Paw ministry has brought in cat food to care for some of the residents' pets, and the Golf Fellowship is offering golf outings for the senior residents. I am thrilled to have had this ministry be given to me as a command from the Lord! I asked the Lord, "Have you called me to this ministry?" He very strongly said in return, "I have commanded you to do it." Since then, I have never looked back.

It may sound like we just go around empowering everyone to start ministries, and while that is a good mindset, there are other options. Many existing ministries or outreaches in communities are already well advanced in serving the public. In some cases, we don't need to reinvent the wheel. Instead, we can encourage our people to work with or partner with existing ministries on a local or even national level. This accomplishes the goal of impacting lives in a tangible way, puts our congregation in contact with pre-believers, and also helps foster unity with other believers. That's another trifecta!

Let's Go There

Besides effecting change in our communities, let's talk about another problem that small groups can help solve while fostering unity with other believers. Pastors can be in a difficult position when speaking out about current social and political issues that affect our communities. The last few years have proven time and again just how polarizing and divisive these topics can be, even in the body of Christ, where we are called to be unified. How do pastors and leaders convey biblical truths to inform their congregations about current real-life concerns without creating additional strife? A sermon series doesn't cut it and may not even be the correct approach.

The complexity of many of these problems and the diversity of views regarding them, as well as potential solutions, don't fit neatly within a 40-minute Sunday morning presentation. Many of these issues need almost constant communication and action to create the momentum necessary to produce community change. However, if we take large amounts of time talking about social matters or politics from the pulpit, we are not bringing all the other life-changing truths of the Bible. It's also not reasonable to address an issue once and expect people to comprehend the information and then move forward to create lasting societal change.

The Lord's Prayer asks that the Father's will be done on earth as it is in heaven (Matthew 6:10). As followers of Jesus, we are called to bring heaven on earth, and that can take many different forms. Where you stand on particular hot-button issues isn't the point; that's between you and

The Outreaching Church

God. My concern is to create a platform to convey biblical wisdom on an ongoing basis that activates people to create biblical change in our communities. That may involve state or national politics, electing community leaders and school boards, protecting the rights of the unborn, tackling issues of inequality, or a host of other things.

We need to have the opportunity to gather and educate people interested in particular topics. Our congregations are looking for biblical wisdom on social issues, and obviously, as expressed in the first chapter, there is no shortage of genuine concerns that the church can give insight on. I'm not here to tell you what you should believe. I am here to encourage sharing wisdom from the Bible and activating people to influence others based on these truths.

Allowing leaders to have small groups around issues that people are seeking more wisdom on is a way to accomplish these goals. In a Constitution small group, for example, people come together and read the Constitution, discuss its meaning, and how to safeguard the rights it creates for our people. Other groups might focus on United States liberty, right-to-life issues to protect the unborn, curriculum taught in public schools, or a myriad of other things. A group focused on state or local politics might create voter guides by asking candidates questions and publishing the results. With this information, people can make informed decisions about which candidates best line up with their values. Some of these outreach groups are connected to national organizations that furnish wisdom, insights, and materials.

One of the groups at our church is Liberty Leaders.

Liberty Leaders seeks to promote and support principled Christian candidates in offices from city councils to governorships and then hold them accountable to work for the people. In the past year, they have held two events per month, with between 80 and 140 people in attendance at each event.

Liberty Leaders

This last election we saw all our candidates get elected in our city. We were able to keep two candidates who openly displayed values that didn't align with scripture out of office. Our local school board was also tipped on the side of Christian candidates. We are holding the line in our community with God's help.

It has been our honor to pray personally for candidates and those at events who are in need of ministry and encouragement. Even those whose views we may not agree with we are open to ministering to. The shift to nonbiblical values in local, state, and national government and in our schools has been so dramatic that it has begun to wake up Christians to be influencers and to bring heaven to earth in the political sphere. While things are very corrupt, we seek to conduct ourselves in a way befitting our Father, whether we agree with individuals or not.

Another group, Community Impact Team, has a mission to serve, equip, and invigorate the local Christian community for success in the areas of freedom, faith, and family. Some of their activities have included distributing "In God We Trust" window stickers throughout the community, creating a voter guide, and participating in the 40 Days of Life campaign to end abortion. The team also builds relationships with local school boards, provides information about bills in the state legislature, and encourages constituents to reach out to their representatives. This group was formed with help from the national organization Family Research Council, which provides training and resources.

Staff Small Groups

Let's look at additional ways small groups strengthen our churches and change our communities. Our church staff can be encouraged to have a healthy attitude of impacting others through small groups. What if every person on your staff built a small group around their job description or gifting? What if this was part of their duties? Those in charge of taking care of the church building and grounds connect with other handymen and women. Musicians have small groups around singing, songwriting, or musical instruments. Tech people work together on apps, social media, security, gaming, or websites.

How about video production? Many people are interested in filming or editing. Why don't we have small groups to connect people in our staff's serving areas? Could there be a group of administrative people? Of course! There is a whole set of thoughts and challenges of project management, stress, and communication that these people face.

Here is the bottom line. Whoever is currently employed at your church will someday not be on staff. Everyone should be training their replacement. So whether they move to a different position, retire, or change careers, they will have built up leaders to fill their shoes. Also, if you continue to connect new people to your congregation, every department will grow, and you will need more staff to handle the growth. These small groups and connections become a practical way to raise up the next generation of leaders for your expansion, additional campuses, or other churches. If we are working with and developing leaders in all areas of our church, do you think it will be any problem to bring on more gifted individuals? Of course not, and now you have an easy process to identify them for ongoing growth.

Here are a few ideas of potential staff groups:

Facilities	Graphics
Mechanical	Decorating
Media	Events
Music	Social Media
Administrative	Hospitality
Video and Photography	

Transitioning Small Groups to Outreach Ministries

In essence, **all small groups should have the mentality of being an outreach ministry.** This is the slight shift in focus many churches need as they develop thriving outreach ministries from an already solid base of small groups. Some of these groups can grow to directly serve their communities in a powerful way. Let's look at a free-market group I lead as an example.

I head up a mountain biking group for advanced mountain bikers. This group meets once a week after work at a different trailhead. The group consists of guys who are very good at mountain biking. For some of you in other parts of the world, mountain bikes are specialized bicycles designed to ride in the mountains. There are electric bikes; however, for our group, we are the motor and also the reason we get up to the top of the hill . . . or not.

This group is a natural for me based on my early years of racing mountain bikes and road bikes around our area. Riding bikes is something I like to do and have a passion for, so I share my hobby with other guys who have a similar interest. I'm not trying to appeal to everyone. The guys who attend have a comparable desire to ride bikes, and the group **fills a need** for camaraderie, to ride hard, and enjoy the outdoors. It also gives us proximity to interact, find out about difficulties going in one another's lives, pray together, and so on.

Obviously, this is a great opportunity for men in our church to come together and share the experience of riding. Perhaps more importantly, it gives us the chance to invite pre-Christian mountain bikers to come out and ride with us. This creates an ideal space for friendship evangelism. We can meet and get to know each other, which could progress to us influencing them for Christ in a myriad of ways.

I just received an email from a man who has never come to our church. He said he can't attend a regular service because he works on Sundays. He had looked at our website and was captivated by the novel idea that a church would promote guys riding mountain bikes. He asked me if he could join us. "Of course, you can! See you Thursday evening after work."

So riding a bike in the mountains, which I totally enjoy, just became an outreach ministry. Shazam! Isn't God good? Who would believe it could be so easy!

Does this only work for mountain biking, or does this also work for golf, frisbee, walking dogs, riding horses, or gardening? Fill in the blank. How can I use my abilities of/interest in_____ through a small group to meet people's needs?

Ask the Right Question

I can already hear some of you protesting. "Mac, I'm overwhelmed. I have zero free time for recreation, downtime, or even to see my family. There is no way I'm going to initiate a small group." I completely understand, and my suggestion to solve your real-life problem would be to . . . start a small group. At this point, most people are scratching their heads and muttering something like, "You must have eaten paint chips as a kid," than reflecting on my mental acuity. Read on.

Let's ask the question, is there any way we can use a small group as a positive answer to one of your life's problems? I work way too many hours, and I get little recreation. I just like working, but I also know I need downtime. So let's ask the right question: How can a small group be a positive factor in my life?

Full disclosure: even though I enjoy mountain biking, and it is very good for me, I won't take time out of my busy life to do it. I have taken zero mountain biking rides this year, even though I enjoy it. The truth is, I won't take the time to stop working and go mountain biking.

This year, my first time in the mountains on a bike was the day my small group started. Last year it was the same way. I started this particular small group to solve my life problem of overworking and not being able to mountain bike. The only way I could justify going was to commit to other guys and use it as an avenue of recreation and ministry together. So think of how a small group could be the answer to one of your life problems.

Busy Parents

What if you are a busy parent with no time to see your children? Why don't you do a group for dads or moms to play at the park with their kids each week? You need a date night with your spouse? So do others! One of our church's largest small groups is a date night for couples. The gathering of couples is huge, and we had to start an additional group just to meet the demand. Whatever you are missing in your life, chances are there is a way to do it and include others.

Do you like gardening and would love some company? Yep, that will work. Congratulations! You have the perfect idea for a small group, solved one of your life problems, and created an avenue for ministry. Do you need to pray more, need help with finances, need a better marriage, need help raising children? A small group can be your answer to these and many more life situations. Most people are looking at their problem, but they are not asking the right questions to solve it. If you ask the wrong question, you get the wrong answer. The right question is, how can starting or attending a small group benefit my life and others?

Do you like to golf? How about fishing, hiking, or a myriad of other fun activities? Now you can use them as a small group and even an outreach ministry. Once again, is this simple or what? It's not only uncomplicated but exciting and fun. Wait a second! I thought ministry had to be complex, tedious, or laborious to be effective? This seems incredibly easy and enjoyable. You're right! It is all those things, and the great news is that God can change our lives and others through small groups.

Outreach Progression

Even though I have no personal desire or calling from God to develop biking into an extensive outreach ministry, almost any group can progress to whatever size and impact the leader is called to. Let's stick with the mountain biking scenario. What if I believed mountain biking was a gift from God for me to use to directly influence a large number of people for Christ? I could gradually recruit a whole team of men and women with a similar perspective. We could purposely develop a gamut of related connection points, including cycling clubs for a range of people from small kids to seniors. Biking and racing for all ages are popular in our community, and there are multiple cycling teams. The legendary Kristin Armstrong, a two-time Olympic cycling gold medalist, is from our city, and there are several other notable successful cyclists in the area as well. The reality is that cycling is incredibly popular where I live.

As a small group, we could pray and brainstorm ideas for serving our cycling community. If we had a lot of great cycling connections and experienced coaches, there are unlimited things we could do. We may decide to initiate a world-class cycling development team for youth. What do you think the outcome would be?

If we cultivate a great program, the results could be a massive following of supportive people with a waiting list of parents wanting to get their kids into our program. This would attract other support, and we could have corporate sponsors willing to help with finances and products. Would this take an immense amount of work to develop? Of course, and it would take even more than that! It would take this being the calling of God on someone's life and the grace of God to complete it. The good news is, there is a myriad of people called and graced by God to meet the needs of society in a variety of ways. We just need to have a foundational structure and process to develop them.

The Outreaching Church

Reflection Questions

1. Reflect on the four steps to move forward with outreach ministries. Start sketching out some ideas about how these steps apply to your situation. (For instance, brainstorm which leaders you could begin moving forward with, or are you that leader? What are the risks involved? How could you mitigate them?)
2. What are some ways that small groups could address social or political issues affecting your community? How could they foster unity with other believers and/or reach pre-believers?
3. What might staff small groups look like in your church?
4. Reflect on the statement, "All small groups should have the mentality of being an outreach ministry." How could this shift in focus impact your small group ministry?
5. How could a small group be a solution to a practical problem you are facing right now?

Chapter 7: What Are You Going to Say?

Pastors, has anyone in your congregation ever approached you with this question? "Pastor, I feel God would have me start _____ ministry. What should I do?" This question can send shock waves of fear through even the most courageous pastors. What would be your answer? What do you think the answer would be from most church leaders if asked this question?

While a hundred mitigating circumstances might affect the response, the question itself puts the pastor in a very precarious position. If the church leader responds with, "Yes! Let's get it started!," they really don't have any clue what they are actually saying yes to, or what the implications are of their commitment to help the ministry succeed. There are already a thousand unknowns, and how is the pastor supposed to manage one more thing when overwhelmed with the daily activities of running a church? There are risks of finances, reputation, relationships, and who knows what else.

The easiest answer is always going to be no or the classic stall tactic, "I'll pray about it," when the real hope is that the person asking the question will forget about it. Unfortunately, it can be hard for someone to forget about something they believe God told them to do. The brush-off is a normal response to something we don't want to deal with in the moment. Isn't that what we do to our kids all the time? When one of them comes to us and says, "Can I go to Tyler's house this weekend? All of our friends are getting together." Our knee-jerk response is no.

It's so much easier than the 26 follow-up questions that have to be asked, like "Who is Tyler? Where does he live? Will his parents be home? How long are you staying? What will you be doing? Who else will be there? Did you get your homework done?" Then there are schedules to be rearranged, the related hassle of trucking the kid back and forth to Tyler's house, and the last-minute request to give one of his friends a ride as well. I'm amazed we ever say yes to anything at all! So, back to the ministry question, with all of its potential hurdles and hassles and headaches, we do our best Nancy Reagan impression from the 80s anti-drug campaign, and we "just say no!"

Do you remember the Dones from chapter two? Maybe their ministry idea got shot down before it ever had a chance to get off the ground, perhaps with a solid no or "That's not who we are; we don't do that here." Or it died the prolonged, agonizing death of being ignored because the pastor didn't have a clue how to facilitate it or safely release the parishioner to try out the idea.

I get it! We answer no because we don't have a structure to help the ministry succeed, or we don't know where it fits within our mission, or how to handle potentially difficult situations arising from the outreach. Perhaps we as church leaders are not well-versed in how to equip the saints for the work of the ministry.

When I talk to pastors, most believe that all ministries need to be under the spiritual covering of a church. This is a biblical as well as practical principle. It provides accountability, support, and wisdom. As I speak with most outreach ministries, they agree that they want to be under the spiritual covering of a church. The problem comes when church leaders have no practical way of facilitating or supporting the ministry. When this happens, those called to the outreach are left to strike out on their own in order to fulfill what God has called them to do.

Because He Didn't Say No

John came up to Pastor Rick in the school gymnasium where the church was meeting and gave him a 13-page, single-spaced description of the ministry he felt God was calling him to start to help hurting and broken people. Pastor Rick's answer? "Great, John—go do it!"[10]

That was in 1991. Since that time, over 27,000 people have gone through Celebrate Recovery at Saddleback

---

10 "History of Celebrate Recovery," Celebrate Recovery, accessed 07/20/2022, https://www.celebraterecovery.com/about/history-of-cr.

The Outreaching Church

Church, the ministry John wanted to start. It is the church's largest outreach, with over 70% of attendees coming from outside of the church. There are now 35,000 churches worldwide using this program to impact their communities, and over five million people have completed a Step Study, one of the core components of the ministry. Celebrate Recovery is being used in prisons, recovery houses, rescue missions, and universities to provide practical help to hurting people and lead them to Jesus. Pastor Rick Warren's decision to say yes to outreach has made Saddleback Church far larger on the outside than it is on the inside, and millions of people have been impacted as a result.[11]

If it hasn't happened yet, it will. Pastor, someone (or maybe several someones) in your congregation is going to say to you: "Pastor, I feel like God would have me start _____ ministry." How are you going to answer? Are you going to say no to something God wants to do, like the next Celebrate Recovery? Or are you going to have the infrastructure in place so that you can say, "Great, go do it!" and have a proven process for them to follow to help God's vision come to fruition?

I'm Not God

Another hesitation pastors might have regarding saying yes to a ministry is, "I don't think that will work. I'm going to say no to save them the heartache of certain failure." Here's

---

[11] "History of Celebrate Recovery."

what I've figured out. I'm not God. I'm not omniscient. I don't know what will work and what won't. Nor did the Holy Spirit give me a cheat sheet about what He is speaking to people in my congregation. Let me give you an example.

A solid Christian woman come up to me and said something akin to, "I don't like people all that much, but I have a passion for animals, and I feel like God wants me to start a ministry to help animals."

What would you tell Kristina, or what would she hear at most churches? Maybe, "Ha! That's funny. Great joke, but we don't preach to housecats here." Or, "We're about saving people. What do animals have to do with that? I don't think that aligns with our mission statement." I have learned I'm not as smart as the Holy Spirit. I don't know what He has spoken to people versus what was a midnight hoagie dream, so my answer is always the same. "Great! Let's see about getting a group going."

Kristina started small, and now her group is a legal non-profit, impacting lives throughout our community. She and her husband Jason specialize in getting high-quality pet food to people who can't afford it. This includes homeless people, low-income shut-ins, and cancer and medical patients. Now she is being asked to bring pets into a hospice care facility as therapy for the patients. What has happened is an incredible ministry that is continually expanding and bringing people into the Kingdom. People believe, "Look, if you care about my dog, you must be a good person, and I will listen to you about other things."

Kristina's Story

God brought forth this passion in me to help others through pets, but I didn't know what to do with it. It wasn't until you [Mac] encouraged me that I started to take steps to put this idea into action.

Our ministry has served as a connection point, providing an opportunity to love and minister to all types of hurting people. We ask the Holy Spirit to lead us in our interactions with the people we meet. In addition to providing tangible support for their pet, we often pray with pet families and tell them that God loves them and their animals.

We have had the opportunity to pray with an owner for healing of his pet's cancer diagnosis. Following the improvement of his pet's condition, the owner stated, "If God loves my dog that much to heal him, then I believe in Him for my own healing." We've ministered to a local veteran struggling with PTSD and social anxiety for many decades, and prayed with a mother still suffering with grief after losing a child 16 years ago. When we saw her again three months later, she said she was doing much better and was on the path to healing.

We also offer financial assistance for emergency medical pet care, and we have helped three separate pet families over the last year with this service. Each family came to us in a time filled with desperation and pain over their suffering pet, and we responded with love and compassion. Each family told us how grateful they were to have a stranger care so much for them and their pet and that our support allowed them to find some peace in an excruciating time.

We are being asked to speak at more and more organizations within the community, and when I introduce myself, I tell them that we are led by God's love for those hurting within our community. I am excited to see what God has planned for our ministry in the coming years. We are currently partnering with three local pet stores that provide food donations, as well as four other local organizations for referrals of those in need.

I can say that God is transforming my own heart through serving others, becoming more comfortable around strangers, growing boldly in faith. I now have love and compassion for the pet owner in addition to the animal—I cry with the owner when they are in pain; I rejoice with them in their victories.

I'm very excited about what this couple and their team are doing. Who knew that loving and caring for people's pets could help us connect people to Jesus? I'll give you one hint: His initials are H. S. Let's talk about the structure that makes this work.

Incubator Groups

We have talked about the power of small groups and how they can be great incubators to launch outreach ministries safely. We have a portion of small groups that we internally classify as incubator groups that could evolve into more substantial outreach ministries. These groups serve a need for the church's attendees and fill a need in our community. These groups have the potential to develop into full-fledged outreach ministries.

There are many advantages to starting these ministries as a small group. As a small group, we can more easily attract similarly gifted people to come together around a function or purpose, which gives them a reason to meet. During this developmental time, it will be natural for the individuals in these groups to pray and start talking about how to serve a segment of society through their abilities and recruit additional like-minded members. This gives us more people to work with, and it safely moves the process forward to build a strong foundation of manpower and increased knowledge.

A huge advantage of these incubator groups is time. Time is passing as they develop a team and the proposed outreach strategy. This gives both the church and the ministry increased security in knowing this was not just a thought that occurred in the middle of the night, but is a gradual, purposefully developing ministry. This should be very comforting to church leadership because the ideas that are moving forward have survived the test of time and have gone through substantial trial-and-error refinement.

Let's say people are interested in ministering to the homeless of our community, and we start a small group. They start talking and praying about the situation, then develop an idea about how to minister to the homeless. The incubator groups are assigned a more seasoned coach to assist them.

After some time of prayer and thought, let's say the ministry decides to have a field trip to try out the ministry idea. One of our groups started out in a very similar manner. The team would meet and make plans; then, on a Saturday, they would take food to the homeless of our community. They tried different locations. They tried various foods, from donuts to peanut butter and jelly sandwiches. They kept experimenting to find out what would work. Pretty soon, they decided to make homemade breakfast burritos and go downtown to a specific area with a large population of homeless people.

What gradually developed is a powerful ministry where thousands of people have been fed physically and many impacted spiritually over the last several years. People have accepted Jesus, gotten jobs, addictions have been broken, and people have become productive members of society. Many of these brothers and sisters in Christ join us at our

The Outreaching Church

Sunday morning worship service every week. All this happened because a few people felt led to pray and took a small step in gathering a small group of people to try out an idea, and the Spirit of God blessed their efforts.

Street Campus Testimony

I've never attended Life Church, but my experience with people from it has been amazing. I'm currently homeless here in Boise, Idaho. Today at the shelter, folks from this church stopped by to bring some well-appreciated breakfast burritos, juice, salsa, prayer cloths, Bibles, and most importantly, compassion.

If folks can come down there on a cold February Saturday, show compassion for others that are in temporary bad/challenging places in life, then that shows true compassion and empathy from members of this church.

I spoke with an incredible lady named XXXX (hope I spelled her name correctly). Just so grateful. Can't wait to attend services at this church. Thank you, folks. God bless you all!

Let's hear from Dave and Jen how this incubator group with such a small beginning has advanced into a 501(c)(3) organization impacting hundreds of people throughout the year.

Dave and Jen

Our team meets at the church every Saturday to prepare 200 breakfast burritos for typically 100 to 150 people per week. We make sure the homeless get at least one hot meal every week while we fellowship, minister, and pray for them.

Here are a few testimonies from the Street Campus.

Through fellowship and prayer, Carla, who had been an addict for over 25 years, gave her life to the Lord and was able to get clean and sober. Now she has a job and is no longer living on the streets.

Cindy from downtown came to church with us, gave her life to the Lord, and eventually was baptized. She was a great influence on others in the homeless community. She rounded people up for church, started a Bible study, and was very bold for the Lord. A month after she was baptized, she unexpectedly passed away, but our team and her son's family have great peace because we know she is celebrating in heaven with Jesus!

Four people last year were able to complete their rehab program. We helped them find jobs; they rented apartments and are no longer on the streets. We also have two more working and almost ready to graduate that have been saving to get into housing. We had 29 salvations and saw 31 people healed in the last year.

The Outreaching Church

Other aspects of our ministry include delivering Christmas cookies and gift bags on Christmas morning and holding a summer Bible study in the park, with plans for additional groups. We also have people on our team who volunteer to transport people on Sundays and Wednesdays who want to attend services. We now have between 10 and 15 people who come to church with us each week. Some are now in rehab programs and have jobs, with hope for a better future.

We are building relationships with homeless shelters downtown and with other programs that assist the homeless community. We continue looking for opportunities to spread the love of Christ to as many people as we can. The passion of our team is to show love and acceptance to people who believe no one cares about them.

Wow, thanks Dave and Jen! That is an exceptional impact for the Kingdom, and it's ongoing and growing!

These incubator groups may need to check local ordinances, get insurance coverage, and definitely keep church leadership informed about what they are planning. After the event, they evaluate the outcome, make any adjustments necessary, continue to pray, and move forward. As this group shows success in serving our community and each other, they can move from being a small group to becoming a ministry outside of the church. These outreach small groups can start as a ministry incubator to bring people together around a problem or need, formulate a Kingdom solution, and develop the steps to move forward to bring His Kingdom to earth.

People who start these groups are mature in God and may have a background in the focus area, favor, or connections, and especially a calling from God that helps them succeed. The overarching component is that they have inward compassion or drive from the Holy Spirit to minister a solution to a particular need in our community. We look for people with the call of God in their life to do a ministry, and we have a structure that can facilitate them succeeding for the Kingdom.

The outreach small groups give individuals a safe process to form a plan and take baby steps to move their ministry ideas from inside to outside the church walls. If things don't work out, it is okay. They can regroup, pray, and try again with increased wisdom and knowledge from their previous efforts. These outreach ministries take the gospel message into our city to solve people's needs.

Ministry Development Path

Before we talk about other possible outreach ministries, let me give you a condensed version of our ministry development path.

1. An individual believes God has called them to develop a ministry.

2. The person starts a small group around a common theme, problem, or area of compassion, attracting others with similar interests.
3. This group of people prays about the problem and possible ministry solutions. They develop some initial ideas and take small steps forward in implementing them. Then they review the results.
4. The group has an assigned coach to help with the process.
5. The ministry gradually refines what it does, and results are continually reviewed.
6. The group progresses to being an outreach ministry.
7. The group can keep growing and moving forward, becoming its own legal entity like a 501(c)(3) nonprofit and forming its own board of directors, as the leaders choose and the Lord leads.

There are significant growth opportunities when you are building outreach ministries from a platform of small groups. A powerful option for outreach leaders is to develop a corresponding separate small group related to the outreach that focuses on discipleship and team growth. For instance, your outreach ministry directly deals with feeding the homeless, repairing homes or cars, or even ministering through horses or other animals. You might consider having a separate small group geared to training and developing the team that will be directly ministering to the public.

This small training group can be a significant first step that allows people to come in, get connected, build relationships, develop skills, and prepare for the ministry aspects of the actual outreach ministry. The group can be an easy access point that anyone interested in serving in the outreach is referred to that meets at regularly planned times and places. Doing so creates a consistent on-ramp for new people to begin volunteering in the ministry. It also gives the outreach leaders a chance to meet, interact with, and get to know new volunteers, creating safety and lowering risk for everyone involved.

We Are Only Limited by Our Imagination

Almost any skill set can be the answer to someone else's prayer. For example, there is a full spectrum of society with little or no clue about mechanical things and have no aptitude for doing repairs. Perhaps they don't have the finances to pay a professional to do the work. This creates an amazing ministry opportunity.

Within your church or community, I can guarantee that there are elderly people with a bucket under their kitchen or bathroom sink to catch dripping water from leaking plumbing. The sad part is that the same bucket has been in the same spot for years with no one to fix this relatively minor problem. If you didn't have the means to fix a leak and you had a bucket under your sink, what would you hope someone would do for you? Perhaps they wish someone would stop by and do a very basic repair, but they don't know who to ask. They may even be praying for a way to get it repaired. What should we be doing for them to show them the love of God?

I can also guarantee there are mechanically minded individuals sitting at home, possibly retired from work, thinking, "God can use the pastor, but I wish he could use me." Is there a way to get these two groups together and seek an answer from God? Of course! When we bring them together, God answers the prayers of both groups, and both groups feel blessed in the process. Serving people doesn't have to be complicated. This double-ended blessing happens because we started a small group around people with abilities to meet someone else's needs. Jesus calls it loving our neighbor.

Neighborhood Prayer

Speaking of neighbors, praying for neighborhoods is an easy place to start that gets people in our congregations into the community. Most churches have people in them with a heart to pray. Do people in our community need prayer, or would they appreciate the thought of someone praying for them? I would say yes and yes. We can start a very simple outreach ministry that utilizes these two basic elements. People who like to pray and walk go down the street, pray for a house, and then place a door hanger on the doorknob that reads something to this effect:

Mac Mayer

Hi Neighbor,

This door hanger is to let you know we came by and prayed for you today. As Christians, we care about the well-being of our neighbors.

God's Blessings,

From your friends at Life Church!

LCboise.com

The door hanger is a subtle approach to telling people they are cared for. We are not even inviting them to church. We are just letting them know someone is interested in their well-being and willing to pray for them. The Holy Spirit can use the door hanger any way He pleases to influence these people for the Kingdom.

This testimony was emailed to our church as a result of this ministry.

"Thanks to your member(s) who placed a 'we prayed for you today' door hanger on our door in the wee hours of the morning this week!!! I found it upon returning from my morning walk at 5:30 a.m. as I was getting ready to start my day, which included caring for my sick family.

The prayers offered on our behalf were God's gift and blessing for me and undergirded us all in difficult days!!! Thanks for the thoughtful mission and ministry your church is engaged in!!!"

The Outreaching Church

You Are Everywhere

I recently asked one new attendee how they heard about our church. Their answer was "You're kidding! I hear about you guys everywhere. I see your bumper stickers, and many of my friends attend your church. I hear about you at work. I hear about you all the time." I want people in communities around the world saying, "Are you kidding? I hear about churches all the time! They are doing great things to help their community."

The physical act of serving our communities is crucial because we tangibly help people with their needs. The great benefit is that it brings us into close proximity with people who have various issues, including the most essential, which is having an eternal relationship with Jesus. When you genuinely care about someone and serve their best interests, you are simultaneously building a solid relationship of trust. It is then an easy transition to share the most significant solution of all, which is Jesus's love for them.

Ministries naturally develop from each other. For example, if you are ministering to people in jail or prison, at some point, they will be released back into society. When they are back in their community, they will need additional help. What will they require to be successful? Celebrate Recovery or other addiction recovery programs, résumé writing, job interview practice, successful dress, marriage skills, and money management are possible ideas. Family or communication skills, parenting classes, job training, employment, housing, medical services, and more are additional areas of need.

As we work with people, we should be aware of other resources they may need. This creates an infrastructure of potential ministry opportunities while simultaneously increasing their potential for success.

A Two-Pronged Serving Connection

Do you think pre-believers would be interested in serving the homeless? That answer would be yes. We discussed the commonalities between the Dones, Millennials, and Z's earlier. These and many others have a similar God-given desire to serve others. You are very likely one of them if you are reading this book. Many of these people are currently pre-saved. We have something they are looking for: a way to serve their fellow men and women. Our attitude is, we can help them serve others, and we don't care if they are currently saved or not. In fact, we are hoping pre-saved people will want to serve with us! Then we can share the love of Christ with the community we're serving and with the pre-saved team members.

One of our groups that feeds the homeless posted pictures on social media of preparing food prior to their outing. This opened a conversation with multiple pre-believers asking how they could help. They asked if we needed dona-

The Outreaching Church

tions of food, money, or equipment; if they could help cook or serve; and how else could they get involved?

These people have an innate desire to do something to benefit others. As discussed in *The Connected Church*, we are looking for ways to connect with all people, including the pre-saved, so we can remove the "pre" and welcome them into the family of God, saved by the precious blood of Jesus. Our answer to the pre-believers that want to help is, "Yes! Of course, you can participate."

While we are connecting with these pre-believers serving right beside us, it allows us to ask questions, find out their needs, and possibly pray for them or be part of God's answer in their life. If we make it a positive experience for them, guess what? They want to come back and serve with us again next week, and the God connection continues. The Holy Spirit is so smart! He arranges these supernatural connections all the time, and lives are changed because of it! Eric's testimony is a real-life example of one of these supernatural God connections with eternal consequences.

José enjoyed serving food to the homeless so much that he invited his unsaved friend Eric to join him. Eric accepted. Eric did not believe that God was there for him. He thought that God was punishing him for the wrong decisions he had made with his life.

In José's words, "After serving this past Saturday, we took Eric out for breakfast and talked to him about Jesus. At the end of the breakfast, I invited Eric to attend church. He was reluctant, but I said we could sit together. Sunday, I met Eric outside the church because he was nervous about going in by himself. I was privately praying for Eric during the service. At the end of the service, Eric responded to the altar call and accepted Jesus as his Savior. I will be inviting Eric to sign up for water baptism this coming Sunday. I will continue to encourage him and connect with him, and the Holy Spirit will lead us to help deepen Eric's relationship with the Lord as a new creation in Christ Jesus!"

This is a typical interaction when we create proximity with pre-believers through acts of service. How well we serve people determines how successful we will be. If we meet people's needs well with the gifts, abilities, and grace God has given us, the groups will naturally grow. More people will be attracted to serve, which results in more people's needs getting met. If we provide people with godly answers, our ministries can't help but grow, and changed lives will be the natural outcome.

If we are ministering to a group of people in need, in all likelihood, they know others in similar life situations. If we are successfully operating, this creates a built-in expansion plan. If I needed help when I came out of prison, and you helped me, I will tell all my friends who will be coming out of jail that you can help them also. If we are serving people

The Outreaching Church

correctly, there will be an ever-expanding realm of new people who can also be ministered to.

Another great thing is that people who have their life changed also want to be part of the solution to help others' lives change. I know I'm that way—how about you? Someone changed our life; wouldn't it be great to pass on the love? The result will be us serving people and helping them have a changed life, resulting in them helping to change more lives, and this will create a continuous landslide of growth for your church and His Kingdom.

Reflection Questions

1. If you are a pastor, have you been asked by a parishioner about a ministry they wanted to start? What was your response? What was the outcome? If you have been on the other side of this equation and felt like God was asking you to start a ministry, what did you do? What was the outcome?
2. Reflect on the idea of small groups as incubators for outreach ministries. What might this look like in your situation?
3. What are some small steps that you or your church body could take to be more active in your community?
4. What are areas of ministry that would be a natural two-pronged serving connection? How could you facilitate this?

Chapter 8: A Scalable Biblical Model

As church leaders and followers of Christ, we understand that we should have outreach ministries. However, there are some inherent problems with the standard approach to developing outreach ministries. Let's delve into these difficulties to better develop a solution. All the ways of creating outreach ministries are not equal. Understanding the challenges and reexamining what the Bible says may lead us to a more efficient, functional paradigm from which to operate. Let's look at issues that can result from developing outreach ministries under the typical mindset of most churches. I may be overgeneralizing, but I want you to understand the problems so together we can find a solution.

First, as we have noted, most churches don't have any outreach ministries, and if they do, the ministry is likely need-based, meaning that it was primarily started to solve a specific need, rather than formed on someone's gifted call of God.

> When people are called by God, they become the owner of the vision.

When people are called by God, they become the owner of the vision. They are not only graced by God to accomplish something, they are also accountable to Him to see it succeed. This is the foundation of our Senior Campus Ministry. Yet the model for many church outreach ministries is program-oriented to meet a need. Let me give you an example.

Someone might believe there is a need for their church to start a school so their children can get a quality Christian education. They don't want to send their kids to schools whose indoctrination is often directly opposed to Christian values. Is this a valid need? Yes, absolutely! Should we open a school? Not necessarily.

Unless we have a gifted leader called by God for its success, I wouldn't recommend it. Is there a difference between someone gifted by God and accountable to Him for developing a school versus someone who isn't called by God and accepts a job? Yes. There is a ginormous difference!

The person who simply accepts a position may or may not be fully committed to the new school's success. If that person leaves, someone else accepts the job and is thrown in to replace them. All the while, the church's leadership is forced to ride shotgun on the entire endeavor. Now multiply this dysfunction by five additional need-based outreach ministries. Can you see how the mental anguish and financial drain on the church are compounding exponentially? (I apologize to some of you who have experienced these results and are now having flashbacks and are running for cover. At least you now know why it happened, and we will discuss ways to avoid these same land mine results in the future.)

Since church leadership is active in the hands-on management of the day-to-day operation of these ministries, this is a huge burden, and it throttles the number of outreaches a church can start. The church is now using large quantities of energy, management, finances, and focus on something they are probably not called to be good at. This is counterproductive because the more outreach ministries we start without a specific leader gifted and called to lead it, **the more inefficient the church is** in managing and overseeing them. The larger the ministry, the larger the drain of manpower and finances. This is not a sustainable model for the church. We can't effectively keep adding ministries under this paradigm.

Fairly soon, the church is overburdened with the responsibility of managing outreach groups, rather than focusing on the biblical mandate to be an equipper of the saints for the work of the ministry, as found in Ephesians 4:11–13. This is a lose-lose scenario. Not only is the growth of outreach ministries stifled, but the pastoral staff is also drawn away from the call of God for their lives—shepherding the flock that God has entrusted to them.

Scalability

In case you missed some of my earlier disclaimers, I'm a business guy. My approach to church growth is largely based on lessons I learned from my years of starting and building companies, and the Bible (as well as the Holy Spirit's brilliant insights). When looking at outreach ministries, I want to know if they are scalable or how we can make them scalable. If you aren't familiar with this term, let me explain.

Scalability is about doing more. It is the ability of a system to handle a growing amount of work by adding resources to it. Ideally, a scalable model sees increasing returns as more capital, labor, and so on are added to it. In economic terms, it means that the cost of each unit produced actually declines as the business expands.

Let's talk about what this looks like in the world of outreach ministries. As we discovered a few paragraphs ago, designing a system in which pastors are responsible for overseeing every aspect of each outreach is not only NOT scalable, it's miserable for everyone involved. Without proper structure, the headaches grow exponentially with the size of the ministry. Is there a different way to develop outreach ministries so the model would be scalable and more ministries could flourish? Scalable in this context means that if we had five ministries, things would work fine, and if we had 55 outreaches, our impact on the market would significantly increase, but our efforts would *not* increase correspondingly.

If we follow the outreach development path outlined in chapter six, we avoid the pitfalls of starting need-based ministries, and better yet, the model is scalable with increasing returns. As more people gifted and called by God step up and start small group incubators to develop their outreach idea, there is an increase in return, that is, lives changed for the Kingdom. There is also an increased commitment by the church, but it is smaller in proportion to the growth that is occurring.

A scalable outreach model is more efficient with Kingdom resources. The "cost" of individual lives changed goes down the larger it gets. The result is that the ministry is changing more lives without an equivalent increase in effort.

Let's look at a scalable business example (franchising) to further illustrate the point. A franchised business is individually owned. This means the local proprietor is wholly responsible for the success of the store he or she invested in. The individual franchise is supported by corporate headquarters, whose primary goal is to equip and serve the franchisee to be successful in serving their community. This is exactly how the small group to full-fledged outreach ministry model works.

Hopefully, I'm making this concept clear. If so, fireworks should be exploding in your brain about the magnitude of how we, as church leaders, can equip and support individually "owned" outreach ministries to do the powerful work of changing lives in our community. The Holy Spirit will be partnering with us every step of the way for maximum success. We will be using the Ephesians 4 mandate for pastors to equip believers to serve and minister to people. The church leadership's responsibility is to provide the growth path, framework, and support for individual outreach ministry leaders to succeed. The success of the ministry itself is the responsibility of that group's leader. This is very similar to corporate headquarters providing tools and support for individually owned franchises to succeed. This is a gigantic paradigm shift in how most churches see and facilitate outreach ministries.

Not to beat a dead horse, but what if the corporation felt like they needed to own and control every aspect of the franchise? This would significantly impede the growth, scalability, quality, and quantity of the community being served. The same problems arise if pastors want to be overly controlling of every ministry launched from the church. If you want a biblically supported discussion of how and why to build an empowerment culture, I recommend reading *The Empowered Church*.

Standards

In case your brain is exploding with destructive bombs instead of happy fireworks as you picture the chaos created by outreaches operating willy-nilly with no oversight, let me talk you off the ledge. I am not suggesting that ministries can just be started and run however they like. Once again, this would be unproductive. With a franchise, corporate headquarters determines what qualifications are needed and who can open one of their stores. There are operational guidelines, training, and agreements in place to ensure that the corporation's standards are upheld. We, as a church, should have policies in place regarding who can start a small group developing into an outreach ministry. This may include discipleship training, serving for a period of time under other ministries, demonstrating mature Christian character—whatever makes sense for you and your church body. What are appropriate operating standards and an agreed-upon statement of faith for ministries under your covering? We can and should put these in place so all parties are protected.

Hold It

I'm sure many of my pastor and church leader friends are freaking out about now. "Mac, hold it! I'm barely getting the sermons done for Sunday, and you are talking about developing an infrastructure to oversee launching abundant outreach ministries? I don't think so."

Take a deep breath and stick with me a few more paragraphs before you jettison the idea.

I understand how you feel. Let me ask you a question. Do you think there are solid, gifted, Christian businesspeople in your church who wish they could use their years of business-building experience for the Kingdom of God? There are many businesspeople who love God and have years of experience building organizations. It would be a dream come true for them, just like it has been for me, to help you build outreach ministries! There is nothing better than using my skill set for Kingdom results, and many others feel the same way. They just need the opportunity.

Pastors, you may be thinking of businesspeople who fit this model. Why don't you do them a favor, give them this book, and see if any of it resonates with them? The church can have a group of gifted support people whose entire role is to help and equip others to build their individual outreach ministries. All parties benefit from the strategic alliance.

Equipping the Saints

If we as church leadership took on the biblical equipping role, what would that look like? To begin with, just having the potential for a ministry to start and a path for it to follow would be a huge win.

If people understand there is a clear path and help for their success, they are far more likely to take steps forward to fulfill the call of God on their life. Many leaders are specifically called and gifted by God on the ministry side. They are the boots on the ground, gifted and trained to do the act of frontline outreach ministry. However, many other skill sets are needed for a full-fledged outreach to be successful. This is where the church leadership team comes in.

The Outreaching Church

Think of all the things that would be necessary for ministries to grow in impact. Volunteer recruiting, volunteer training, website development, grant writing, vision casting, social media, management skills, administrative functions, organizational development, and the list goes on and on. What if we created and outlined a division of labor between the two parties: the outreach ministry and an administrative team supporting all the outreach ministries? Then the outreach ministry team could work in what they excel at (the specific act of service), and we have a gifted volunteer/paid support team, working in what they are called to (supporting the work of the ministry). This creates a strategic alliance where each party works in their giftings for the outreach's overall success, and lives are changed for the Kingdom. This, in effect, is equipping the saints for the work of the ministry.

As the church provides a volunteer on-ramp for people to be connected to a ministry and various services that will help the ministry grow, the outreach is free to focus its energies where they should be—directly connecting, ministering, and serving people. This becomes a scalable model that has unlimited ministry potential. There is almost no limit to the number of ministries people can start and the number of lives we can impact. The support team can add members as they are needed. This strategic alliance creates a God-gifted life change in our communities.

Some support areas can be facilitated by the church and some by the group itself. We as the church may be able to build teams of people who are also working in their giftings to help the ministries through coaching, leadership, marketing, grants, and so on. With this model, we can develop **a church larger on the outside of our walls than on the inside.** This will result in the inside of the church being strong, healthy, and thriving. The whole body of believers will be functioning together to impact our community for Christ.

The following are some thoughts regarding possible responsibilities and the relationship between the church and the outreach ministry. This separation of responsibilities is invaluable, especially when dealing with potentially thorny social or political issue groups.

Church/Leadership Responsibility

1. Create a culture and opportunity for success.
2. Provide exposure of the ministry.
3. Establish an on-ramp for volunteers to connect.
4. Encourage the development of layers of leadership.
5. Provide coaching for the leadership.
6. Look for opportunities to help the ministry.

Ministry Responsibility

1. Commit to fulfill God's calling.
2. Take the lead and responsibility for the ministry's success.

3. Connect with and serve both believers and pre-believers.
4. Serve and disciple both believers and pre-believers.
5. Raise up replacement leaders.
6. Look for opportunities to connect to other ministries.
7. Abide by the church's statement of faith.
8. Provide evidence of insurance that names the church as an additional insured if needed.

Favoritism

Here is a common question that I get almost every time I talk with outreach ministries. The conversation goes something like this. "We want to know if the church leadership or the senior pastor really believes in the importance of what we are doing. We would like him/her/they to acknowledge us and help us grow our ministry. After all, our outreach involving politics, voting, protecting the unborn, sex trafficking, sexual identity, school, missions, the homeless, the elderly, (fill in the blank) is the very heart of God. So, can we get special recognition?"

I understand the question, and I'm so thankful the leaders feel like their ministry is one of the most important. This sentiment reveals the passion of the Holy Spirit for what they are doing, and this is exactly what they should believe. Obviously, this is also a loaded topic and one we should talk about. We have discussed the importance of free-market small groups that create innovation, so let's stay with this analogy.

I may ask the leaders if they believe in the concepts of free enterprise as connected to free-market small groups. In a true free-market system, the overseeing government (or church leadership) creates equal opportunity for *all* enterprises. The government should not advocate or show favoritism for certain businesses. The governing body is to provide a level playing field and equal opportunity for people to start and operate their endeavors.

If the governing body promotes some activities over others, this erodes equal opportunity. In terms of the church, there are some ministries with more potential for impact, but it is the leadership's responsibility to create equal opportunity and pathways for success for all groups.

Just as within the free-enterprise system there are laws for companies and organizations to follow, so should the church follow ethical guidelines of operation. I believe it is the church's responsibility to equip the saints for the work of ministering and serving the needs of our community. The church can provide a free-market structure where these ministries can be developed. The ministries that are best at serving the needs of their community will flourish, and the ones that aren't meeting needs well may want to consider restructuring or closing. I hope this is not too direct, but I want people to look to God for wisdom in successfully serving their fellow man and not to church leadership for favoritism.

The Outreaching Church

Nonprofits

Some of your outreach ministries may eventually mature and become legal nonprofits. These organizations will develop a clearer vision and assemble a board to direct and oversee their activities. My viewpoint is that we want outreach ministries that are growing to be individually owned by the person with the vision and not owned, operated, or controlled by the church. There are several reasons for this.

First, if a ministry stops, needs money, or loses a leader, it is not the church's responsibility to step in and take it over. Will the church be there to help guide, counsel, and lead, or possibly provide money? Absolutely, but it is not the church's responsibility to make every ministry work. Our responsibility is to create a healthy culture where people graced by God can start a ministry and succeed in what He called them to do. It's their responsibility to make it happen. If it fails, it fails. I'm okay with that because it is not my calling or obligation to make every individual ministry succeed.

Do I want it to flourish? Of course, but, everyone has their own decisions, and their problem is not mine. Hopefully, this isn't too harsh! If it is, as a Christian, you have to forgive me. Ha! The second reason the church should not own the ministry is because there are times when the ministry may feel they would be better off outside of our spiritual church umbrella of help and support. If so, they need the freedom to leave. It could be because the leadership may have failed to serve them properly—or they may have outgrown the structure of the church. It is not about my ego that these ministries must be affiliated with our church. It is about the ministry of God succeeding for the Kingdom, and if they can build their outreach better by not affiliating with us, they should leave. The great news is that this also keeps us as leaders in a serving position to help them succeed. I'm not building my kingdom or ego. I'm building His Kingdom. This is how servant leaders think.

Funding

Will money be needed for some of these outreach endeavors? Yes. The good news is that most groups need little or no funding to start. As outreaches grow, money can become a factor. Even more great news is that God has abundant resources to see His will accomplished. God is not out of ideas or money to creatively build ministries. From my vantage point, people graced to build a ministry receive resources from God to succeed.

I love the saying, "If it's God's will, it's God's bill." If He wants it done, finances won't be a factor. This truth doesn't mean we do nothing. However, it is often an advantage if ministries do not get easy money from someone else. Not having easy money keeps us as prayerful good stewards, seeking God for guidance to best use the resources we do have.

The Outreaching Church

For an example of the opposite, think about the enormous waste and inefficiency of big government programs. These organizations effortlessly misuse taxpayers' money In an endless array of ridiculous, careless ways. My experience is that when we are good stewards and doing God's will, people and companies are drawn to help us succeed, including supplying finances. Many companies are looking to partner with or give money, donations, food, equipment, and the like if we are doing good things for society.

Recently our ministry that feeds the homeless got a $10,000 check from a local grocery chain. There were no strings attached; they just liked what we were doing by feeding the homeless. As previously noted, local pet stores are helping to provide food supplies to Kristina's ministry to local pet families. Many corporations are glad to give food and supplies to organizations making a tangible difference in people's lives.

I like teaching, "The biggest problem with nonprofits is that they act like nonprofits." If a nonprofit is not run professionally, including being good stewards and operating to the highest levels of accountability, problems can happen. It can also be an issue for nonprofits to continually look outside themselves for finances to solve their problems. "If someone will just give us money, we can grow" is the utterly wrong viewpoint. More money may result in a bigger mess if the issue is with management and allocation of existing resources.

The Law of Exchange says that people want to spend their resources where they will get the best return. This applies to how people and companies use their finite supply of money, and it also applies to how people spend their limited time volunteering. If donors do not feel like they are getting a good return on their investment, or they feel as if those resources are being wasted, they are not likely to continue to give.

There is not a general shortage of money, but there is a shortage of great ideas. Great undertakings are like a magnet, and money is drawn to them. A potential source of funds for some of these ministries is financial grants. If they are run professionally and are impacting lives, there may be grant money available for their growth from various sources. Ministries should have such a compelling true story of how lives are effectively being impacted that people are almost demanding to help them with money and resources to be part of the success.

Focusing on how we are tangibly changing lives is the right thing to do, regardless of how difficult it may be. The alternative is holding out our beggar's cup and hoping people will feel sorry for us and toss in a quarter. Let's produce real results, and the money will take care of itself.

Church Connection

As outreach ministries grow, they will hopefully look to connect with other churches doing some sort of related ministries. Our prayer is to have the whole body of Christ stand up and take its proper place in society. I'm not interested in just our church's growth. I'm interested in the success of all churches that proclaim Jesus as Lord. All our outreach ministries can be looking for things they have in common with other ministries in order to team up for greater impact. There is no sense in us duplicating the efforts of one another.

For example, suppose there is a church or food bank with an abundance of food and another team that is already ministering to the homeless community. By putting their areas of expertise and calling together, they can more effectively minister to people in need and multiply their impact. Other examples would be a church with a prison ministry working with churches that have well-developed addiction recovery groups or entrepreneurs interested in building felon-friendly businesses where people coming out of jail can be employed.

We are called to unite as the body of Christ, and coming together in a strategic alliance to build outreach ministries is a great way to do it. If there are areas in which we can work together with other churches to multiply our impact, let's do it! It is in everyone's best interest to team up and bring our specializations together, so His Kingdom is populated. Let's pray and act in unity with the rest of the body of Christ and provide answers to the world's problems.

Reflection Questions

1. Have you been involved in need-based ministry outreaches versus ones that were started because of a particular gifting and calling of God on an individual? What was that experience like?
2. If your church has outreach ministries, is the pastoral staff heavily involved in managing them? How is this working? Are there benefits or drawbacks to the approach?
3. How can the church more effectively provide support and structure for outreach ministries without directly taking responsibility for them and their success? What are small steps you could take in this direction?
4. Reflect on the relationship between outreach ministries and the church/leadership as outlined in this chapter. Does it seem reasonable? Would this delineation of responsibilities work in your situation? Why or why not?
5. What opportunities do you see where you can partner with other ministries in your community? How could you move these relationships forward and foster more unity in the body of Christ?

Chapter 9: Get in the Game

Many Christians are in the game of changing lives for the Kingdom. Unfortunately, many more are sitting on the sidelines as spectators, wrongly believing they are unimportant, while their lives pass them by. These camped-out nonparticipants may think there is no way for them to use their abilities for the Kingdom. They could also view accomplishing at their jobs and businesses, being financially stable, buying new homes and cars, and taking vacations as equivalent to the ultimate of all success. It isn't. Ultimately, worldly success can come at a very high price if we aren't investing the talents Jesus gave us for Kingdom return.

Life is full of mirages. We have all watched the movie scenes of exhausted desert travelers who think they see a watery oasis ahead. They use the last of their energy to struggle to get there, only to find out it is a false goal and a dry, waterless wasteland. How does this mirror many of our lives as we continually chase one material success after another? "I need a bigger house. Okay, now a second home in the woods. We need a vacation at an expensive amazing destination. I also need a boat to enjoy the lake. On second thought, we need a house with plenty of ground, so we can have more family time. Now that we have the ground, we need a tractor and a bunch of other equipment to take care of it."

Whether it's vehicles or homes or vacations or hobbies, there is always something new and better, shiny objects to pursue that keep us from God's plan for our life. "Yes, but I will be satisfied when I get (fill in the blank)." Sorry to say, we will never find true fulfillment through material accomplishments. They are just mirages. Lasting satisfaction cannot come from accumulating stuff. It didn't work for Solomon, and it won't happen for us either.

> Whether it's vehicles or homes or vacations or hobbies, there is always something new and better, shiny objects to pursue that keep us from God's plan for our life.

Let's reflect on all the achievements you have attained so far. Did any of them give you lasting contentment? Shocker. Guess what? They didn't for me either. These accomplishments usually resulted in a temporary bump of satisfaction, but the price I paid for them was extraordinary. I traded a segment of my finite life span.

You've heard it said before: time is the most precious commodity on earth. Just ask a billionaire with failing health what they would trade for more time. We take the most important thing at our disposal—our life—and exchange it for trinkets. We accomplish something that doesn't really fulfill us, so we do the same thing repeatedly, winding up at one mirage after another.

Junkyard Bucket List

I can remember devoting my finite life energies toward

the temporary enjoyment of cars, homes, and expensive trinkets, but I was still unfulfilled. I call all my worldly success a junkyard bucket list. All the cars, houses, motorcycles, motorhomes, and toys I spent my life pursuing all ended up in a junkyard. What about you? Do you have a junkyard bucket list? I could rationalize and justify the list of things keeping me from fulfilling God's will for my life. It's embarrassing to think about how much energy I wasted on those fleeting worthless endeavors. But here's the great news! The game isn't over. I'm still breathing. I can redirect my life energies from mirages to a real Kingdom oasis, and so can you.

I believe we can find fulfillment, but as the writer of Hebrews tells us, we need to "throw off everything that hinders and the sin that so easily entangles. And let us run with perseverance the race marked out for us" (12:1, NIV). It is up to us to get rid of anything impeding us from completing what God has called us to do. Those shiny objects we chase might not be outright sinful, but they can certainly be a snare if they take our attention off what God has entrusted for us to accomplish. We end up paying a very high price for those short-term trinkets.

Many of us have been frustrated that we couldn't find a significant way to serve God. Yes, we have attended church, and yes, we have given money, but we've always thought, isn't there more? We are right! We are all gifted by God with particular strengths, and these aptitudes are the answer to someone else's prayer. Our abilities are the reason others are drawn to us. We have their answer.

Using our God-given talents to solve a need in people's lives creates proximity, and proximity creates the possibility for influence. This influence helps people find their answers and can also be a part of the Holy Spirit's equation to bring Jesus into their lives. The Holy Spirit is doing a mighty work, and it is an honor for us to partner with Him for Kingdom impact. As a result of this partnership, we find fulfillment and accomplish the ultimate success for our life, "Well done, thou good and faithful servant," while His church is enlarged both inside and out.

Coming Full Circle

Remember the question I asked when we started our journey together? If you only had one prayer to change the world, and the answer was guaranteed, what would it be? My prayer is that the body of Christ would step up and take its proper place of serving people, using our God-given gifts to change the world.

We have reflected that the answer to the desperate state of the world is for us as Christians to stand up and take our place. People are gifted by God and have a vision to reach out to others, but they need a path to fulfill His call on their lives. They become the leaders, the most critical component to helping a ministry flourish. We, as a church, provide the operating structure for the ministry. The system with the most advantages, free-market small groups, is incredibly flexible, allowing connection points around any number of interests that are not contrary to the Bible or our church culture.

Free-market groups gather people around a common problem-solving subject or function. Just as businesses that serve others well will flourish, small groups that help people well will also grow. If groups are not successful, they can change their content to better serve the public or stop and start another group.

Starting outreaches as free-market small groups considerably lowers risk of failure. Using the passage of time to its full advantage, we can observe the ministry as it slowly develops. The small group structure serves as an incubator from which full-fledged outreach ministries develop. They are also an effective environment for ministering to pre-saved team members. As the groups thrive, they can gradually evolve to serve the community at large on a broader scale. Some of these ministries will gradually develop into legal nonprofits.

The responsibility of church leadership is to help these outreaches succeed in ministering to the community. Our job is to equip the saints for the work of the ministry. As a leadership team, we can recruit gifted people to serve as a support structure in areas of finances, marketing, training, and so on. This model creates a scalable solution where many outreaches can be started based on God's calling on individuals in the church. The results of developing an outreaching church are that many people's gifts are activated for Kingdom purposes. We are developing a church larger on the outside than it is on the inside.

Now more than ever, we need people to take their place as part of the active functioning body of Christ for the last days' impact. We need every person connected, every part operating as it was designed to do (Ephesians 4:16). Let's make sure we are connected to our calling, and we are actively helping others to do the same. This is vital for Kingdom success. Will you join me and others on this incredible once-in-a-lifetime adventure connecting as the body of Christ and influencing lives to change the world?

mac

P.S. Mac Mayer Ministries would like to continue to help you on your journey of success. We have several resources available to help you discover your calling and guide you in the process of understanding your abilities and how they relate to a market need. These resources are available by emailing me at mac@macmayer.com.

The Outreaching Church

Reflection Questions

1. Where are you in the game of changing lives for the Kingdom?
2. What is your junkyard bucket list?
3. Are there weights you need to throw off to run your race for the Kingdom more effectively? What are they and what are some steps that you are going to take in this area?

Mac Mayer

The Outreaching Church

www.ingramcontent.com/pod-product-compliance
Lightning Source LLC
Chambersburg PA
CBHW070158100426
42743CB00013B/2966